ROUGH GUIDES

T0082313

POCKET ROUGH GUIDE
LISBON

written and researched by
MATTHEW HANCOCK
with additional material by Amanda Tomlin

CONTENTS

LISBON

Set across a series of hills overlooking the broad estuary of the Rio Tejo (River Tagus), Lisbon's stunning location and effortless beauty immediately strike most first-time visitors. It's an instantly likeable place, a big city with a population of around two million, but one that remains human enough in pace and scale to be easily taken in over a long weekend. That said, many visitors visit again and again, smitten by a combination of old-world charm and cosmopolitan vibrancy that makes it one of Europe's most exciting cities.

View of Lisbon from Cristo Rei

What's new

Due to Covid-19, many smaller cafés, restaurants and hotels were forced to close down, but we have refreshed our listings with many venues that have survived the pandemic. In addition, we highlight the best places to go in the fashionable district of Intendente just north of the centre (see page 77). Once the haunt of the down-at-heel, it is now a hub of exciting new bars and restaurants. We also review the new Treasury Museum in Ajuda, showcasing the Portuguese Crown Jewels.

Although one of the EU's least expensive capitals, Lisbon was once one of the continent's wealthiest, controlling a maritime empire that stretched from Brazil to Macau. The iconic Torre de Belém, Mosteiro dos Jerónimos and dramatic Moorish castle survive from these times, though many other buildings were destroyed in the Great Earthquake of 1755. Today, much of the historic centre – the Baixa, Chiado and Bairro Alto – dates from the late eighteenth and nineteenth centuries. The biggest attraction in these quarters is the street life: nothing beats watching the city's comings and goings from a pavement café over a powerful *bica* coffee or Portuguese beer.

If you're fit enough to negotiate its hills, Lisbon is a great place to explore on foot: get off the beaten track and you'll find atmospheric neighbourhoods sheltering aromatic *pastelarias* (patisseries), traditional shops, and shuttered houses faced with beautiful *azulejo* tiles. Getting around by public transport can be fun in itself, whether you're cranking uphill on one of the city's ancient trams, riding a ferry across the Rio Tejo, or speeding across town on the metro, whose stations are decorated with adventurous contemporary art.

Lisbon also boasts excellent museums – from the Gulbenkian, with its amazing collection of arts through the ages, to the Berardo, whose modern paintings are the envy of Europe, via the Museu Nacional de Arte Antiga, the national gallery, with top Portuguese and European masterpieces.

Lisbon's eclectic nightlife scene ranges from the traditional fado clubs of the Alfama district to glitzy venues in the Bairro Alto and along the riverfront, many of them playing African and Brazilian beats influenced by immigrants from Portugal's former colonies.

Elsewhere, the city offers a pleasing mishmash of the

Best places for alfresco dining

The best way to soak up Lisbon's atmosphere is to grab an outdoor table and sit back with a coffee or something more substantial. Sample tapas at *Pharmacia Felicidade*, with a fine little garden overlooking the Tagus (see page 66), or enjoy a pizza-with-a-view at riverside *Casanova* (see page 46). It's hard to find a lovelier lunch spot than the sleek, riverside *Á Margem* (see page 89). Alternatively, head to one of Lisbon's squares or *miradouros* (viewpoints), many of which have cafés, bars or restaurants, such as *Portas do Sol* (see page 49).

Portas do Sol restaurant

traditional and modern: chequered-tiled bars full of old-timers supping brandies adjacent to boutiquey clubs pumping out the latest sounds; tiny *tascas* with bargain menus scrawled in white chalk on boards rubbing shoulders with gourmet restaurants eyeing the latest Michelin awards, and artisanal stores that wrap purchases in paper and string sitting alongside malls packed with high-street and designer stores.

Should city life begin to pall, take the train out to the beautiful hilltop town of Sintra, whose lush, wooded heights and royal palaces comprise a UNESCO World Heritage Site. Alternatively, the lively resorts of Estoril and Cascais are just half an hour away, with the best beaches lying south of the city, along the Costa da Caparica, where Atlantic breakers crash on kilometre after kilometre of superb dune-backed sands.

When to visit

Lisbon is comfortably warm from April to October (average daily temperature 20–28ºC), with cooling Atlantic breezes making it less hot than Mediterranean cities on the same latitude. Most Lisbon residents take their holidays in July and August (27–28ºC), which means that some shops, bars and restaurants close for the period and the local beaches are heaving. Lower temperatures of 22–26ºC mean September and October are good times to visit, as is June, when the city enjoys its main festivals. Even in midwinter it is rarely cold and, as one of Europe's sunniest capitals, the sun usually appears at some stage to light up the city.

Where to...

Shop

Suburban Lisbon has some shopping malls, but the city centre is a pleasing mix of quirky local stores and independent outlets. The top end of **Avenida da Liberdade** features the likes of Armani and Louis Vuitton, and Chiado is the place to head for glass and jewellery. Antique shops cluster round **São Bento**, **Príncipe Real** and **Campo de Santa Clara**, while off-the-wall clothing and accessories are to be found in the boutiques of the **Bairro Alto**. **Santos** is the design district of design and the go-to for contemporary jewellery and homeware.

OUR FAVOURITES: Manuel Tavares, see page 32. Embaixada, see page 64, Ler Devagar, see page 81.

Eat

You're never far from a restaurant in Lisbon. For diversity, head to the **Bairro Alto** district where you'll find an eclectic array of inexpensive diners alongside ultrahip venues. The **Baixa** caters to Lisbon's workers and has a whole street, Rua das Portas de Santo Antão, largely given over to seafood restaurants. International flavours can be sampled by the Tejo at the **Parque das Nações** and the dockside developments at **Santa Apolónia** and **Doca de Santo Amaro**, while fashionistas head to the cool haunts of **Cais do Sodré**. Some of the best dining experiences, however, are in local neighbourhood restaurants highlighted in the Guide.

OUR FAVOURITES: Mercado da Ribeira/Time Out Market, see page 51, Mini Bar, see page 65, O Barbas, see page 122.

Drink

The most historic cafés are scattered throughout the **Baixa** and **Chiado** districts, where you'll find locals getting their caffeine fixes throughout the day. You can also get beer, wine or food at these places, though many bars only open after dark (see pages 35 and 56). Portuguese beers – largely Sagres and Super Bock – are inexpensive and recommended, while local wines are invariably excellent. Worth sampling too are local brandies; the white variety of port, which makes an excellent aperitif; and a powerful cherry brandy called *ginginha* – several bars in the Baixa specialize in the stuff.

OUR FAVOURITES: Chapitô, see page 48. Park, see page 69, Portas Largas, see page 69.

Go out

Lisbon has a pulsating nightlife, with the highest concentration of clubs and bars in the **Bairro Alto**. Many locals prefer the less frenetic vibe of the **Cais do Sodré** district, which has a handful of cool clubs and happening bars; while the city's biggest clubs are to be found near the river, especially *LuxFrágil* near **Santa Apolónia** and the upmarket venues of **Alcântara**. There are various excellent live music venues, with the **Bairro Alto** and **Alfama** famed for their *fado* houses.

OUR FAVOURITES: Casa Independente, see page 48, Pink Street, see page 53, Hot Clube de Portugal, see page 101.

Lisbon at a glance

◁ Sintra see page 108.
With its fairy-tale palaces, the hilltop town of Sintra is a must-see day-trip from the capital.

Avenida, Parque Eduardo VII and the Gulbenkian see page 90.
The grand Avenida da Liberdade leads to the leafy Parque Eduardo VII; beyond, the Gulbenkian displays an extraordinarily rich collection of ancient and modern art.

◁ The Lisbon coast see page 118.
In less than an hour you can reach superb beaches at Estoril, Cascais or south to Caparica, famed for its surf and miles of sands.

Estrela, Lapa and Santos see page 70.
Well-to-do Estrela and Lapa boast gardens and excellent museums, while earthy Santos is the riverside district of design.

Belém and Ajuda see page 82.
Many of Portugal's maritime explorers set sail from Belém, home to some of the city's finest monuments and museums.

Doca de Alc

Alcântara and the docks see page 76.
Lisbon's docks shelter appealing riverside bars, clubs, restaurants and a couple of top museums.

| 0 | metres | 500 |
| 0 | yards | 500 |

▷ **Parque das Nações** see page 102.
This futuristic park occupies the former
Expo '98 site, with a range of modern
attractions including a huge oceanarium.

Ⓜ

Bairro Alto and São Bento see page 58.
The Bairro Alto, or Upper Town, shelters the city's
best restaurants, bars and clubs, a short walk from
the parliament building at São Bento.

Ⓜ

Ⓜ

The Sé, Castelo and Alfama see page 36.
Next to the Sé cathedral, Alfama is an ancient
warren of steep streets leading up to the
city's stunning Moorish castle.

Ⓜ

Ⓜ

Ⓜ

Ⓜ

Ⓜ

Ⓜ

Ⓜ

Ⓜ

Ⓜ

Ⓜ

Ⓜ

Chiado and Cais do Sodré see page 50.
Lisbon's upscale shopping area, Chiado,
rubs shoulders with down-to-earth Cais
do Sodré, site of the main market.

N

The Baixa and Rossio see page 24.
The heart of the modern city, an elegant
grid of eighteenth-century streets
running down to the River Tejo.

15

Things not to miss

It is not possible to see everything that Lisbon has to offer on one trip – and we don't suggest you try. What follows, in no particular order, is a selection of the city's unmissable highlights, including fascinating museums, historical buildings, and custard tarts to die for.

< **Museu Calouste Gulbenkian**
See page 95
Virtually an A–Z of the history of art, from the Mesopotamians to the Impressionists, all set in delightful gardens.

∨ **A night out in Bairro Alto**
See page 67
The 'high district' is a grid of streets filled with the city's biggest concentration of restaurants, bars and clubs.

< **Praça do Comércio**
See page 24
The city's grandest square, beautifully arcaded and facing the Tagus.

∨ **Oceanário**
See page 103
This spectacular oceanarium has a massive central tank and is home to all kinds of marine creatures, from sea otters to sharks.

THINGS NOT TO MISS

∧ **Mercado da Ribeira (Time Out Market)**
See page 51
Part colourful fruit, veg and fish market and part vibrant food hall packed with stalls selling all kinds of dishes and drinks.

< **Museu Nacional de Arte Antiga**
See page 71
Portugal's national gallery includes works by the likes of Nuno Gonçalves and Hieronymus Bosch.

∧ A ride on a tram
See page 137
The vintage trams are the best way to negotiate Lisbon's steepest gradients and narrow, cobbled streets.

∨ Pink Street
See page 53
This is the place to be seen in the evening, filled with clubs, hip bars and *fado* joints.

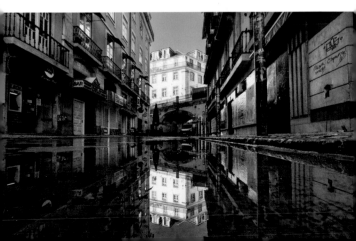

∧ Torre de Belém
See page 86
An iconic Lisbon building, this fabulously ornate tower was built to defend the mouth of the Rio Tejo.

< Pastéis de Belém
See page 89
Head to this famous *pastelaria* for the best custard tarts in town.

< **A day out in Sintra**
See page 108

A UNESCO World Heritage Site, this attractive wooded hilltop town was the summer retreat for Portuguese royalty whose fabulous palaces can still be visited today.

∨ **A day at the beach**
See page 118

It's just a short hop from Lisbon to some excellent Atlantic beaches: those at Cascais and Estoril are easiest to reach.

THINGS NOT TO MISS

Day One in Lisbon

Confeitaria Nacional. See page 34. Start the day with a punchy *bica* coffee in one of Lisbon's most historic cafés, where the decor is as alluring as the pastries.

The Baixa. See page 28. Head down main Rua da Augusta and explore the lively streets and cafés of the Baixa grid.

Chiado. See page 50. Stroll up Rua do Carmo and Rua Garrett where many of Lisbon's best shops can be found.

Armazéns do Chiado shopping centre

Lunch. See page 56. Try *Leitaria Académica*, with a simple menu and tables outside a lovely square.

Tram #28. See page 43. This is Lisbon's most famous tram route, grinding back through the Baixa and up towards the Castelo through the Alfama.

Castelo de São Jorge. See page 40. Walk up to the ruined Moorish castle, the heart of historic Lisbon.

Alfama. See page 43. Take the steps into the Alfama, Lisbon's village within a city where traditional life still holds sway.

Museu do Fado. See page 44. Gain an insight into the history and sounds of Portugal's distinctive music at this informative museum.

Tram #28

Dinner. See page 49. Try one of the Alfama's fado houses, where you can dine while listening to live music; *A Baiuca* is a good place to start.

Drinks. See page 49. End the night by the riverside at *Lux*, one of Europe's coolest clubs.

Museu do Fado

Day Two in Lisbon

Museu Calouste Gulbenkian. See page 95. Take the metro to this superb museum displaying arts and crafts from the time of the Ancient Egyptians to the French Impressionists.

Parque Eduardo VII. See page 95. It's a short walk from the museums to Lisbon's main central park famed for its *estufas* – hothouses filled with exotic plants.

Praça do Comércio. See page 24. Take the metro or bus to the city's graceful riverside square and take the riverside path west for ten minutes to Cais do Sodré.

Lunch. See page 51. Have lunch at one of the many food stalls in the Time Out Mercado da Ribeira, Lisbon's main market.

Mosteiro dos Jerónimos. See page 83. Take the tram to Belém's fantastic monastery, built to give thanks to the success of Portugal's great navigators.

Berardo Collection. See page 85. Don't miss this superb collection of modern art, featuring the likes of Andy Warhol and Paula Rego.

Torre de Belém. See page 86. Climb the elaborate sixteenth-century riverside tower that has become the symbol of the city.

Dinner. See page 64. Eat at *1 de Maio*, a traditional restaurant serving inexpensive Portuguese staples.

Drinks. See page 67. Stick around the Bairro Alto and wait for the nightlife to crank up at its hundreds of little bars and clubs.

Museu Calouste Gulbenkian

Greenhouse garden in Parque Eduardo

Praça do Comércio

Lisbon viewpoints

Built on seven hills, Lisbon has some fantastic *miradouros*, or viewpoints, each with its own distinctive outlook over the city's skyline – here we list the best.

Miradouro de Santa Luzia. See page 40. The best place to see over the terracotta rooftops of the Alfama and the eastern riverfront.

São Vicente de Fora. See page 42. Climb to the top of this historic church for dizzying views over the eastern city from its extensive roof.

Castelo de São Jorge. See page 40. Not quite Lisbon's highest hill, but climb around the ramparts to see all sides of the city.

Parque Eduardo VII. See page 95. The top of the park offers an exhilarating panorama encompassing Lisbon and beyond.

🍴 **Lunch.** See page 101. Chill out by a lake at *A Linha d'Água*, which serves good-value buffet lunches at the top of the park.

Miradouro da Graça. See page 42. Superb views over the Castelo and the city beyond can be had from this breezy terrace by the church of Graça.

Miradouro de São Pedro de Alcântara. See page 58. A broad, tree-lined viewpoint from where you can gaze down on the Baixa and the castle opposite.

Miradouro de Santa Catarina. See page 59. Tucked-away *miradouro* with sweeping views over the Tejo, a popular hangout for Lisbon's alternative crowd.

🍴 **Dinner.** See page 67. *Noobai* is hidden under the lip of Miradouro de Santa Catarina and serves inexpensive food and drinks.

Cityscape from Miradouro de Santa Luzia

View from São Vicente de Fora

Linha d'Água

Lisbon for families

Lisbon is very family-friendly and children are welcomed everywhere. Below are some of the best attractions for those with kids of any age.

Street lifts. See page 50. There are several wacky street lifts up Lisbon's steepest hills; Elevador da Bica is the most fun.

Oceanário. See page 103. One of the largest oceanariums in Europe, this stunning building has sharks, rays, otters, penguins and fish galore.

Pavilhão do Conhecimento. See page 102. This science museum has fantastic hands-on experiments and challenges for people of all ages, together with informative exhibits.

🍽 **Lunch.** See page 107. The traffic-free restaurants of Parque das Nações are great for kids – for an inexpensive lunch try the popular *ZeroZero* pizzeria.

River cruises. See page 138. Take a leisurely cruise up the Tejo to see the city from the river.

Museu da Marioneta. See page 72. From medieval marionettes to contemporary satirical puppets, this museum trumpets an art form that satisfied children long before computer games.

Museu da Carris. See page 78. Lisbon's trams are great fun to ride on, but here kids can clamber about trams, buses and metro trains with fewer crowds.

Caparica. See page 121. Lisbon's best beaches are just south of the city, great at any time of the year for a walk or day by the sea.

Sintra. See page 108. Horse and carriage rides, castles and fantasy palaces make this a great day out.

🍽 **Dinner.** See page 32. Spacious, early-opening *Bom Jardim* has tables inside and out and affordable food that kids love.

Elevador de Santa Justa

Museu da Marioneta

Parque das Nações

PLACES

Bronze fountain, Rossio

The Baixa and Rossio

The tall, imposing buildings that make up the Baixa (Lower Town, pronounced bye-sha) house some of Lisbon's most interesting shops. With plenty of hotels and guesthouses, this is also the tourist epicentre, whose needs are served by a range of cafés, restaurants and street entertainers. Facing the river, this area felt the full force of the 1755 earthquake that destroyed much of what was then one of Europe's wealthiest capitals. The king's minister, the Marquês de Pombal, swiftly redesigned the sector with the grid pattern evident today, framed by a triangle of broad squares. Praça do Comércio sits to the south, with Praça da Figueira and Rossio to the north, the latter having been the city's main square since medieval times.

Praça do Comércio

MAP P.26, POCKET MAP E13

The beautiful, arcaded **Praça do Comércio** represents the climax of Pombal's design. Its classical buildings were once a royal palace and the square is centred on an exuberant bronze equestrian statue of Dom José, monarch during the earthquake and the period of

the capital's rebuilding. Two of Portugal's last royals came to a sticky end in this square: in 1908 King Carlos I and his eldest son were shot dead here, clearing the way for the declaration of the Republic two years later.

The square has been partly pedestrianized in recent years in a successful attempt to make it more

Aerial view of Praça do Comércio

Rua Augusta

tourist-friendly, with a panoply of cafés and shops on either side. The secluded Patio da Galé, tucked into the western arcades, hosts frequent events, while the **Torreão Poente**, at the southwest corner of the square, is part of the Museu de Lisboa and hosts temporary exhibits – see Ⓦ bit.ly/Torreao. The north side of the square is where you can start tram tours of the city. However, it is the square's riverfront that is perhaps most appealing, especially in the hour or two before sunset, when people linger in the golden light to watch the orange ferries ply between the Estação Fluvial ferry station and Barreiro on the other side of the Tejo. An attractive walk is to head west along the pedestrianized riverfront to Cais do Sodré (see page 50).

Lisbon Story Centre

MAP P.26, POCKET MAP E13
Praço do Comércio 79 Ⓜ Terreiro de Paço
Ⓦ lisboastorycentre.pt, charge.
This is the highlight of a group of touristy cafés and shops that fill the square's historic eastern arcades.

The **Lisbon Story Centre** gives a potted, visual account of the city's history – good for a rainy day, though somewhat pricey. There are six zones, each dedicated to a phase in Lisbon's past. The multimedia displays include models, paintings, photos, narrations and filmed re-enactments – the highlight is a somewhat gory 4D film depicting the 1755 earthquake, and a "virtual" scale model of the modern city.

Arco da Rua Augusta

MAP P.26, POCKET MAP E13
Ⓜ Terreiro de Paço Ⓦ bit.ly/ArcoDaRua, charge.
Praça do Comércio's most prominent building is a huge arch, the **Arco da Rua Augusta**, adorned with statues of historical figures, including the Marquês de Pombal and Vasco da Gama. Acting as a gateway to the city, the arch was built to celebrate Lisbon's reconstruction after the earthquake, although it wasn't completed until 1873. You can take a lift up to just below the Clock Room, a small

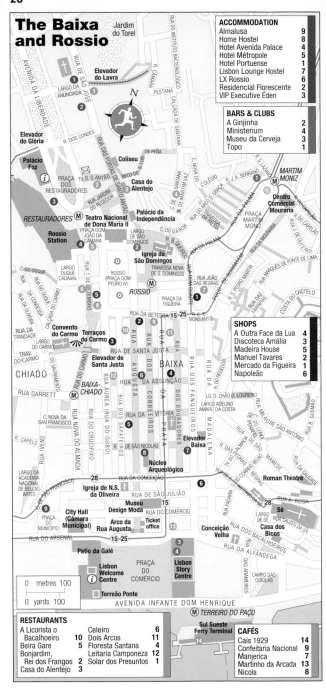

The Baixa and Rossio

Jardim do Torel

exhibition space centred round the workings of a nineteenth-century clock. From here, you can squeeze up a spiral staircase to the flat roof of the monument where you'll be greeted by unmissable views across the Praça do Comércio and the Baixa. Don't be tempted to stand under the bell here – when it strikes, you'll regret it.

Rua Augusta
MAP P.26, POCKET MAP D11

Completely paved in mosaics, the broad **Rua Augusta** runs from Praça do Comércio up to Rossio and is the Baixa's main pedestrianized thoroughfare. Filled with shops, market stalls and touristy restaurants, it can get pretty packed, but its buskers and street performers are always entertaining.

Museu Design Moda
MAP P.26, POCKET MAP E13
Rua Augusta 24 Ⓦ mude.pt, currently closed for renovation and due to re-open end of 2023.

Housed in a grand former bank, the **Museu Design Moda** is an impressive collection of around 2,500 design and fashion classics from the 1930s to today, amassed by former stockbroker and media mogul Francisco Capelo. The museum's ever-changing exhibitions include design classics, such as furniture by Charles and

Historic café Martinho da Arcada

Ray Eames and Phillipe Starck, and also features Capelo's fashion collection – haute couture from the 1950s, 1960s street fashion and the brand labelling of the 1990s. Look out for Ron Arad's "Big Easy" steel chair (1951), Frank Gehry's wiggle chair (1972) and the 1959 Vespa, while fashionistas will adore Paco Rabanne's metalized leather boots, Pierre Cardin's 1950s coats and Alexander McQueen's superb fur skirt. There's also a first-floor shop and top-floor café/restaurant.

The Lisbon earthquake

Early eighteenth-century Lisbon had been one of the most active and important ports in Europe, making the Great Earthquake of 1755 all the more tragic. The quake, which was felt as far away as Jamaica, struck Lisbon at 9.30am on November 1 (All Saints' Day), when most of the city's population was at Mass. Within the space of ten minutes there had been three major tremors and the candles of a hundred church altars had started fires that raged throughout the capital. A vast tidal wave later swept the waterfront and, in all, 40,000 of the 270,000 population died. The destruction of the city shocked the continent and prompted religious debate between philosophers Voltaire and Rousseau. For Portugal, it was a disaster that ended its capital's golden age.

Praça do Município

MAP P.26, POCKET MAP D13

The attractive, mosaic-paved **Praça do Município** houses the Neoclassical nineteenth-century Câmara Municipal (City Hall), where the Portuguese Republic was declared in 1910, flatteringly described by one of Portugal's greatest poets as "one of the finest buildings in the city". The square adjoins Rua do Arsenal, an atmospheric street lined with pungent shops selling dried cod and grocers selling cheap wines, port and brandy.

The Baixa Grid

MAP P.26, POCKET MAP D11-12

Pombal designed **the Baixa** to have three main streets dissected by nine smaller streets. Many of these streets took their names from the crafts and businesses carried out there, like Rua da Prata (Silversmiths' Street) and Rua dos Sapateiros (Cobblers' Street). Modern banks and shops have disturbed these divisions somewhat, though plenty of traditional stores remain; the central section of Rua da Conceição, for example, is still lined with shops selling beads and sequins. Some of the most interesting streets to explore are the smaller ones running south to north – Rua dos Correeiros, Rua dos Douradores and Rua dos Sapateiros. Pombal also wanted the grid's churches to blend in with his harmonious design, so much so that they are almost invisible – walk along Rua de São Julião and the facade of the church of Oliveira is barely distinguishable from the offices alongside it, though its tiled interior is delightful.

Núcleo Arqueológico (NARC)

MAP P.26, POCKET MAP E12
Rua dos Correeiros 21 Ⓦ bit.ly/NARCLisbon, hourly tours, advance bookings required, free.

Recently renovated, one of Lisbon's smallest but most fascinating museums lies beneath the streets of Baixa. The remains of Roman fish-preserving tanks, a fifth-century Christian burial place and Moorish ceramics can all be seen in the tiny **Núcleo Arqueológico** containing the remains of excavations revealed during building work on the BCP bank. Most exhibits are viewed through glass floors or from cramped walkways under the modern bank during a 50-minute tour (tours leave on the hour and alternate between English and Portuguese). Pombal actually rebuilt most of the Baixa on a

---

Fernando Pessoa

Martinho da Arcada, the café at the north end of Praça do Comércio, was the favoured haunt of Fernando Pessoa (1888–1935), Portugal's greatest contemporary poet and a leading figure of twentieth-century modernism. Born in Lisbon, Pessoa grew up in South Africa before returning to Portugal in 1905 to work as a translator. He spent much of his time composing poems in Lisbon's cafés. Many of his works are about identity – he wrote under various alter-egos or "heteronyms", each with their own personality and style. The most famous are Alberto Caeiro, Ricardo Reis and Alvaro de Campos, though his most famous work is the *Book of Disquiet* written under the heteronym Bernardo Soares. The partly autobiographical work is full of extraordinary philosophical ruminations that have established his reputation as a leading existentialist artist.

Exhibits in Núcleo Arqueológico

riverbed, and you can even see the wooden piles driven into the waterlogged soil to support the buildings, the same device that is used in Venice.

If you're interested in discovering more about Lisbon's underground ruins, ask the museum about early summer visits to the amazing Roman tunnels that lie beneath the Baixa. Access is restricted to the 2,000-year-old tunnels, whose purpose remains unclear, because they are usually flooded. As a result they are open for just three days a year and attract enormous queues. It's a bizarre sight watching people enter the tunnels, which can only be accessed through a manhole cover between tram tracks on Rua da Conceição.

Elevador de Santa Justa

MAP P.26, POCKET MAP D11
Rua de Santa Justa, charge.
Raul Mésnier's extraordinary and eccentric **Elevador de Santa Justa**

was built in 1902 by a disciple of Eiffel. Its giant lift whisks you 32m up the inside of a latticework metal tower, to deposit you on a platform high above the Baixa. Before taking the upper exit on to the Largo do Carmo, head up the dizzy spiral staircase to the pricey rooftop café with great views over the city.

Rossio

MAP P.26, POCKET MAP C11
Praça Dom Pedro IV (popularly known as **Rossio**) has been the city's main square since medieval times and it remains the hub of commercial Lisbon. Its central space sparkles with Baroque fountains and polished, mosaic-cobbled pavements. During the nineteenth century, Rossio's plethora of cafés attracted Lisbon's painters and writers, though many of the artists' haunts were converted to banks in the 1970s. Nevertheless, the outdoor seats of the square's remaining cafés are

perennially popular meeting points. On the northwestern side of the square, there's a horseshoe-shaped entrance to Rossio station, a mock-Manueline complex with the train platforms an escalator ride above the street-level entrances.

Teatro Nacional de Dona Maria II

MAP P.26, POCKET MAP D10
Rossio ⓦ tndm.pt.

Rossio's biggest concession to grandeur is the **Teatro Nacional de Dona Maria II** built along its north side in the 1840s, and heavily restored after a fire in 1964. Inside there is a good café. Prior to the earthquake, the Inquisitional Palace stood on this site, in front of which public hangings and *autos-da-fé* (ritual burnings of heretics) took place.

Igreja de São Domingos

MAP P.26, POCKET MAP D11
Largo de São Domingos ☎ 213 428 275.

The **Igreja de São Domingos** stands on the site of the thirteenth-century Convento de São

Praça dos Restauradores

Domingos, where sentences were read out during the Inquisition. The convent was destroyed in the earthquake of 1755, though its portal was reconstructed soon after as part of the current Dominican church. For over a century it was the venue for royal marriages and christenings, though it lost this role after the declaration of the Republic and was then gutted by a fire in the 1950s. Some say the fire purged some unsavoury acts that took place on the spot, such as the massacre of forcibly converted Jews (known as "New Christians") which began here in 1506. It was reopened in 1997 after partial restoration to replace the seats and some statues; however, the rest of the cavernous interior and the scarred pillars remain powerfully atmospheric.

Praça da Figueira

MAP P.26, POCKET MAP D11

Praça da Figueira is a historic square (once the site of Lisbon's main market), though the unfortunate addition of an underground car park has detracted from its former grandeur. Nevertheless, it is slightly quieter than Rossio, and still offers appealing views of the green slopes of the Castelo de São Jorge.

Praça dos Restauradores

MAP P.26, POCKET MAP C10

The elongated **Praça dos Restauradores** (Square of the Restorers) takes its name from the renewal of independence from Spain in 1640. To the north of the square, the **Elevador da Glória** offers access to the Bairro Alto (see page 58); south sits the superb Art Deco frontage of the old Eden cinema, now an apartment-hotel (see page 127). The square is dominated by the pink Palácio de Foz on the western side, built for a count in 1777 and housed the Ministry of Propaganda under the Salazar regime (1932–74). It is now

Casa do Alentejo

home to the Portuguese Tourist
Office (see page 141). Its ornate
mirror room hosts occasional
concerts.

Rua das Portas de Santo Antão

MAP P.26, POCKET MAP D10

The pedestrianized **Rua das
Portas de Santo Antão** is well
known for its seafood restaurants.
Despite the tourist trappings on
this and the adjacent Rua Jardim
Regedor (you're likely to get
waiters trying to smooth-talk you
into their premises), it is worth
eating here at least once to sample
its seafood. The street is also
home to several theatres, and the
domed **Coliseu dos Recreios** at
#96 (Ⓦcoliseulisboa.com), which
opened in 1890 as a circus but is
now one of Lisbon's main concert
venues.

Casa do Alentejo

MAP P.26, POCKET MAP D10
Rua de Santo Antão 58 Ⓜ Terreiro de Paço
Ⓦcasadoalentejo.pt, free.

A cultural centre with its own
café-bar and restaurant (see page
32), the **Casa do Alentejo** is a

sumptuously decorated pseudo-
Moorish palace, little changed for
decades. Originally a seventeenth-
century mansion and later a casino,
it has been a centre dedicated to
culture from the Alentejo district
since the 1930s. You can just
wander in and look around the
beautifully tiled interior – some
of the tiles are from the original
mansion – but most visitors head
upstairs to the dining room or
café-bar, with its neighbouring
ballroom, an amazing, slightly
rundown room hung with
chandeliers.

Elevador do Lavra

MAP P.26, POCKET MAP K5
Largo da Anunciada, charge.

Rua das Portas de Santo Antão
ends next to where another of the
city's classic *elevadores*, **Elevador
do Lavra**, begins its ascent. The
funicular opened in 1884 and is
Lisbon's oldest and least tourist-
frequented *elevador*. At the top a
short walk down Travessa do Torel
takes you to **Jardim do Torel**, a
tiny park above a series of ornate
terraces offering exhilarating views
over the city.

Shops

A Outra Face da Lua

MAP P.26, POCKET MAP E12
Rua da Assunção 22.

This buzzy space specializes in retro fashion – fab vintage clothes, tin toys and the like; it also has a great attached café serving burgers and snacks.

Discoteca Amália

MAP P.26, POCKET MAP D11
Rua Áurea 272.

A small but well-stocked shop named after famous fado singer Amália Rodrigues, with a good collection of traditional Portuguese fado music. If you're looking for a recommendation, the English-speaking staff are usually happy to help.

Madeira House

MAP P.26, POCKET MAP D12
Rua Augusta 133.

As you'd expect, linens and embroidery from Madeira feature, along with some attractive ceramics, tiles and souvenirs from the mainland.

Manuel Tavares

MAP P.26, POCKET MAP D11
Rua da Betesga 1a.

Small treasure-trove dating from 1860, with a great selection of nuts, chocolate and national cheeses, and a basement stuffed with vintage wines and ports, some dating from the early 1900s.

Mercado da Figueira

MAP P.26, POCKET MAP E11
Praça da Figueira 10b.

The decorative, narrow entrance hall gives onto a well-stocked supermarket with a good array of inexpensive wines, ports and fresh produce and its own café.

Napoleão

MAP P.26, POCKET MAP E12
Rua dos Fanqueiros 68–70.

This spruce shop offers a great range of quality port and wine from all Portugal's main regions, and its enthusiastic, English-speaking staff can advise on what to buy.

Restaurants

A Licorista o Bacalhoeiro

MAP P.26, POCKET MAP D11
Rua dos Sapateiros 222–224 ☏ 213 431 415.

This pleasant tile-and-brick restaurant is a popular lunchtime stop, when locals flock in for inexpensive set meals or mains such as *bacalhau à brás*. €€

Beira Gare

MAP P.26, POCKET MAP D11
Praça D. João de Câmara 4 ☏ 213 420 405.

Well-established café/restaurant opposite Rossio station, serving stand-up Portuguese snacks and bargain meals. Perch at the bar if the tables are full. Constantly busy, which is recommendation enough. €

Bonjardim, Rei dos Frangos

MAP P.26, POCKET MAP C10
Trav de Santo Antão 11–18 ☏ 213 424 389.

A bit of a Lisbon institution thanks to its spit-roast chicken, and now so popular that it has spread into three buildings on either side of a pedestrianized alley. There are plenty of tables outdoors too. A half-chicken is the dish to go for, though it also serves other meat and fish at less generous prices. €

Casa do Alentejo

MAP P.26, POCKET MAP D10
Rua das Portas de Santo Antão 58
ⓦ casadoalentejo.pt.

A centre dedicated to Alentejan culture (see page 31), with its own restaurant, in a beautifully tiled upstairs dining room. Alentejo specialities include rice with lamb and mushrooms and *carne de porco à alentejana* (grilled pork with

Casa do Alentejo

clams); or just pop in for a drink in the superb bar or courtyard taverna. €€

Celeiro

MAP P.26, POCKET MAP D11
Rua 1° de Dezembro 65 Ⓦ celeiro.pt.
Just off Rossio, this inexpensive self-service restaurant sits in the basement of a health-food supermarket and offers tasty vegetarian spring rolls, quiches, pizza and the like. There's also a streetside café offering snacks and drinks. €

Dois Arcos

MAP P.26, POCKET MAP D11
Rua dos Douradores 163 Ⓣ 218 879 689.
The 'two arches' is one of the more historic restaurants on this Baixa street with historic prices too: simple, well-prepared grilled meat and fish dishes, such as salmon steaks and generous portions of *febras* (pork steaks). €€

Floresta Santana

MAP P.26, POCKET MAP D10
Calçada Santana 18 Ⓣ 963 945 338.
A short (uphill) walk from the bustle of the Baixa, but a world away in terms of atmosphere, excellent-value meals are served in a friendly, family-run place which gets busy at lunchtimes. The fish and meat are fresh and generous, and desserts are home-made and huge. €€

Leitaria Camponeza

MAP P.26, POCKET MAP D12
Rua dos Sapateiros 155–157 Ⓣ 923 132 488.
Formerly a *leitaria* (dairy shop) and still displaying the Art Nouveau decor from its past existence, this is now a simple restaurant with a short, moderately priced menu – the meat *espetadas* (skewers) are particularly good. €€

Solar dos Presuntos

MAP P.26, POCKET MAP J5
Rua das Portas de Santo Antão 150
Ⓦ solardospresuntos.com.
The "Manor House of Hams" is, not surprisingly, best known for its smoked ham from the Minho region in northern Portugal, served cold as a starter. There are also excellent, if expensive, meat and seafood dishes, many using traditional recipes. Popular with celebrities, it's best to book a table. €€€

Confeitaria Nacional

Cafés

Cais 1929

MAP P.26, POCKET MAP F13
Estação Sul Sueste, Terreiro do Paço ☎ 911 929 276.

Part of the beautiful Arc Deco Sul Sueste ferry terminal – which now acts as a base for boat tours – *Cais 1929* sits in a 1930s *building* recently renovated by architect Ana Costa. Most people are lured by the outdoor seating, right up by the waterfront, a great spot for a coffee, drink or snack. €€

Confeitaria Nacional

MAP P.26, POCKET MAP D11
Praça da Figueira 18B.

Opened in 1829 and little changed since, with a stand-up counter selling pastries and sweets below mirrors and stucco ceilings. There's a little side room and outdoor seating for sit-down coffees and snacks. €

Manjerica

MAP P.26, POCKET MAP E11
Rua das Regras 5A.

This simple café with a few outdoor tables serves a good range of vegetarian and vegan dishes at very good prices and is a good destination for breakfast, brunch or lunches. Expect the likes of pancakes, banana bread, toasties, eggs benedict and scrambled tofu. €

Martinho da Arcada

MAP P.26, POCKET MAP E13
Praça do Comércio 3.

One of Lisbon's oldest café-restaurants, first opened in 1782 and declared a national monument in 1910. It has been a gambling den, a meeting place for political dissidents and, later, a more reputable hangout for politicians, writers and artists. It is now divided into a simple stand-up café and a slightly pricey restaurant. The outdoor tables under the arches are a perfect spot for a coffee and a *pastel de nata*. €€

Nicola

MAP P.26, POCKET MAP D11
Rossio 24–25.

The only surviving Rossio coffee house from the early twentieth century, once the haunt of some of Lisbon's great literary figures. The outdoor tables overlooking the bustle of Rossio are the best feature,

A starter for ten euros?

At restaurants, don't feel you're being ripped off when you're served an array of starters before you even order your main course, then get a bill for what you've eaten at the end. This is normal practice in Portugal and no waiter will take offence if you politely decline whatever you're offered. Starters can vary from simple bread, butter and olives to prawns, cheeses and cured meats. If you're tempted, it's a good idea to ask the waiter how much each item costs. Check your bill, too, to ensure you've not been charged for anything you declined.

though it has sacrificed much of its period interior in the name of modernization. €

Bars

A Ginjinha

MAP P.26, POCKET MAP D11
Largo de São Domingos 8.
Everyone should try *ginjinha* –
Portuguese cherry brandy – once.
There's just about room in this
microscopic joint to walk in, down
a glassful and stagger outside to see
the city in a new light.

Ministerium

MAP P.26, POCKET MAP E13
Ala Nascente 72, Praça do Comércio
Ⓦ ministerium.pt.
The grand and historic buildings
of the former Ministry of Finance
partly make up the stylish backdrop
to this hip club mostly playing
house and techno and attracting
top-name DJs. There's a spacious
dance floor plus quieter zones and a
great rooftop café-bar if you get the
munchies – check the website for
events and parties.

Museu da Cerveja

MAP P.26, POCKET MAP E13
Terreiro do Paço Ala Nascente 62–65.
Undoubtedly touristy but
indisputably fun, this bar-
restaurant serves not bad food, but
most people visit to sample some of
its 100 beers, sourced from around
the country and Portugal's former
colonies. Try some of the highly-

rated craft beers such as Sovina
from Porto or letra from Braga,
inside or out on its tables on the
square. If you want to learn more
about the history of Portuguese
brewing, *visit the upstairs museum*
(charge).

Topo

MAP P.26, POCKET MAP E10
Sixth floor, Centro Comercial Martim Moniz,
Praça Martim Moniz Ⓣ 215 881 322.
Set on the top floor of a shopping
centre, this contemporary bar-
restaurant has great views towards
the castle from both the light
and airy interior and its outdoor
terrace. The drinks and cocktail
list is as long as the bar, and it also
serves light snacks or pricier mains.
At weekends there are often DJs.

Historic Nicola coffee house

The Sé, Castelo and Alfama

East of the Baixa, the streets climb past the city's ancient cathedral, or Sé, to the dramatic remains of the Castelo de São Jorge, an oasis of tranquillity high above the city. East of the castle lie two of Lisbon's most prominent churches, São Vicente de Fora and Santa Engrácia. The districts around the castle – Mouraria, Santa Cruz and particularly the Alfama – represent the oldest and most atmospheric parts of Lisbon, served by famous tram 28, which wends its way round the castle and down to the fashionable district of Intendente. Down on the riverfront, Santa Apolónia, the international train station, is situated by the riverfront that boasts the glitzy *Lux* club, while a little further east lies a historic steam pumping station and a surprisingly fascinating tile museum.

The Sé

MAP P.38, POCKET MAP F12
Largo da Sé, Tram #28 ☎ 218 566 752, charge.

Lisbon's main cathedral, **the Sé**, was founded in 1150 to commemorate the city's Reconquest from the Moors on the site of their main mosque. It's a Romanesque structure with a suitably fortress-like appearance. The great rose window and twin towers form a simple and effective facade, although there's nothing particularly exciting inside: the building was once splendidly embellished on the orders of Dom João V, but his Rococo whims were swept away by the 1755 earthquake and subsequent restorers. All that remains is a group of Gothic tombs behind the high altar and the decaying thirteenth-century **cloister**, currently closed for archeological excavations which have revealed the remains of a sixth-century Roman house and Moorish public buildings.

The Baroque **Treasury** (charge) holds a small museum of treasures including the relics of St Vincent, brought to Lisbon in 1173 in a boat that was piloted by ravens, according to legend. Ravens were kept in the cloisters for centuries afterwards, but the tradition halted when the last one died in 1978. To this day, the birds remain one of the city's symbols.

Igreja de Santo António and Museu Antoniano

MAP P.38, POCKET MAP E12
Largo S. António da Sé 22, Tram #28 ☎ 218 860 447.

The small eighteenth-century church of **Santo António** (open daily) is said to have been built on the spot where the city's most popular saint was born as Fernando Bulhões; after his death in Italy in 1231 he became known as St Anthony of Padua. The tiny neighbouring **museum** (charge) chronicles the saint's life, including his enviable skill at fixing marriages, though only devotees will find interest in the statues and endless images.

Casa dos Bicos

MAP P.38, POCKET MAP F13

Rua dos Bacalhoeiros 10 Ⓦ bit.ly/
CasaBicosLisbon, charge.
The **Casa dos Bicos** means the
"House of Points", and its curious
walls – set with diamond-shaped
stones – give an idea of the richness
of pre-1755 Lisbon. It was built in
1523 for the son of the Viceroy of
India, though only the lower facade
of the original building survived
the earthquake. It is now owned by
the Saramago organization, which
uses the venue for recitals and a
permanent exhibition dedicated
to the Nobel Prize in Literature
winner and Portuguese author José
Saramago, who died in 2010.

The ground floor has been
maintained as an archeological area
where you can view sections of a
third-century Roman wall and fish-
processing plant, excavated from
beneath the building.

Museu do Aljube – Resistência e Liberdade

MAP P.38, POCKET MAP F12
Rua de Augusta Rosa 42 Ⓦ museudoaljube.
pt, charge.
This small but engaging and
moving **museum** is dedicated

to **resistance and freedom**,
commemorating those who have
been censored or repressed, in
particular people who risked their
lives during the dictatorship of
Salazar (1926–68). Housed in a
former political prison, it details
the drastic and often brutal lengths
Salazar's regime went to hold onto
its former colonies and preside over
an increasingly weary population
up until the 1974 revolution.
Exhibits over three floors include
old photos and newsreels, radio
broadcasts and personal statements
from people who were imprisoned
here, including Mário Soares (later
the Portuguese president) and
author Miguel Torga – you can also
go inside their former windowless
cells, just one by two metres in size.

Museu do Teatro Romano

MAP P.38, POCKET MAP F12
Entrance on Patio de Aljube 5, Tram #28
Ⓦ bit.ly/TeatroLisbon, charge.
The **Museu do Teatro Romano**
displays a wealth of Roman coins,
spoons and fragments of pots,
statues and columns excavated
from the ruins of a Roman

Quirky Casa dos Bicos

38

THE SÉ, CASTELO AND ALFAMA

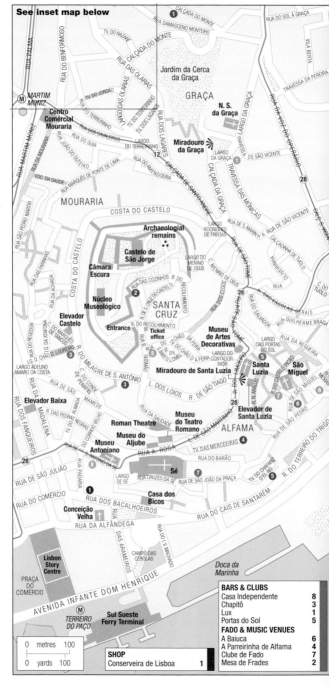

BARS & CLUBS

Casa Independente	8
Chapitô	3
Lux	1
Portas do Sol	5

FADO & MUSIC VENUES

A Baiuca	6
A Parreirinha de Alfama	4
Clube de Fado	7
Mesa de Frades	2

SHOP

Conserveira de Lisboa	1

The Sé, Castelo and Alfama

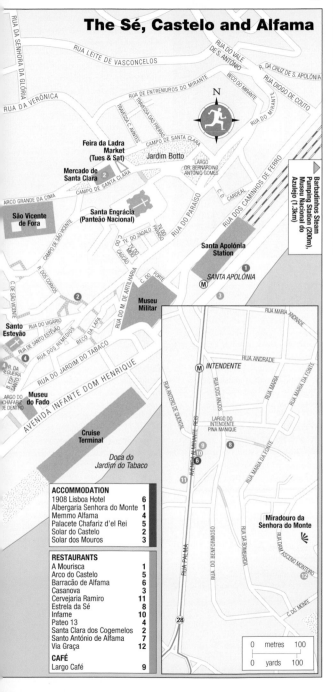

ACCOMMODATION

1908 Lisboa Hotel	6
Albergaria Senhora do Monte	1
Memmo Alfama	4
Palacete Chafariz d'el Rei	5
Solar do Castelo	2
Solar dos Mouros	3

RESTAURANTS

A Mourisca	1
Arco do Castelo	5
Barracão de Alfama	6
Casanova	3
Cervejaria Ramiro	11
Estrela da Sé	8
Infame	10
Pateo 13	4
Santa Clara dos Cogemelos	2
Santo António de Alfama	7
Via Graça	12

CAFÉ

Largo Café	9

Museu de Artes Decorativas

theatre, dating from 57 AD, which are fenced off just north of Rua Augusto Rosa. Roman Lisbon – Olisipo – became the administrative capital of Lusitania, the western part of Iberia, under Julius Caesar in 60 BC, and the theatre shows the wealth that quickly grew thanks to its fish-preserving industries.

Miradouro de Santa Luzia

MAP P.38, POCKET MAP F12

The church of Santa Luzia marks the entry to the **Miradouro de Santa Luzia**, a spectacular viewpoint where elderly Lisboetas play cards and tourists gather to take in the sweeping views across the Alfama and the river beyond.

Museu de Artes Decorativas

MAP P.38, POCKET MAP F11
Largo das Portas do Sol 2, Tram #28 or #12 Ⓦ fress.pt, charge.

Set in the seventeenth-century Azurara Palace, this fascinating **museum** contains some of the best examples of sixteenth- to eighteenth-century applied art in the country. Founded by a

wealthy banker and donated to the nation in 1953, the museum boasts unique pieces of furniture, major collections of gold, silver and porcelain, magnificent paintings and textiles. The rambling building covers five floors, set around a stairway decorated with spectacular *azulejos*. Highlights include a stunning sixteenth-century tapestry depicting a parade of giraffes, beautiful carpets from Arraiolos in the Alentejo district, and oriental-influenced quilts that were all the rage during the seventeenth and eighteenth centuries. The museum also has a small café with a patio garden.

Castelo de São Jorge

MAP P.38, POCKET MAP F11
Bus #37 from Praça da Figueira Ⓦ castelodesaojorge.pt, charge (includes visit to Câmara Escura and Núcleo Museológico).

Reached by a confusing but well-signposted series of twisting roads, the **Castelo de São Jorge** is perhaps the most spectacular building in Lisbon, as much because of its position as anything else. Now Lisbon's most-visited tourist site, the castle was once the heart of a walled city that spread downhill as far as the river. The original Moorish castle on this site was besieged in 1147 by a particularly ruthless gang of Crusaders who, together with King Alfonso I of Portugal, conquered Lisbon after some four hundred years of Moorish rule. Badly damaged during the siege, its fortifications were rebuilt. From the fourteenth century, Portuguese kings took up residence in the old Moorish palace, or Alcáçova, within the walls, but by the early sixteenth century they had moved to the new royal palace on Praça do Comércio. Subsequently, the castle was used as a prison and then as an army barracks until the 1920s. The walls were partly renovated by Salazar in the 1930s and further restored for Expo '98. A series of gardens, walkways and **viewpoints** hidden within the old Moorish walls makes this an enjoyable place in which to wander about for a couple of hours, with spectacular views over the city from its ramparts and towers.

Câmara Escura

MAP P.38, POCKET MAP F11
Castelo de São Jorge, charge (included in visit to Castelo de São Jorge).

One of the castle towers, the **Tower of Ulysses**, now holds a kind of periscope which projects sights from around the city onto a white disc with commentary in English. Unless you like being holed up in dark chambers with up to fifteen other people, though, you may prefer to see the view in the open air.

Núcleo Museológico and Archeological Remains

MAP P.38, POCKET MAP F11
Castelo de São Jorge, charge (includes visit to Castelo de São Jorge and Câmara Escura).

Only a much-restored shell remains of the old Moorish Alcáçova. This now houses the **Núcleo Museológico**, a small museum containing items unearthed during excavations in the castle, including Moorish lamps, Roman storage jars and coins, and pottery and tiles from the seventeenth century. Included in the ticket price is a 15-minute guided tour of the **Archeological Remains**, an excavation site that includes the scant remains of an Iron Age house, an eleventh-century Moorish quarter and the ruins of the fifteenth-century Palácio dos Condes de Santiago, built for the Bishops of Lisbon.

Santa Cruz and Mouraria

MAP P.38, POCKET MAP F11
Crammed within the castle's outer walls, but free to enter, is the tiny medieval quarter of **Santa Cruz**. This remains a village in its own right, with its own school, bathhouse and church. Leaving Santa Cruz, a tiny arch at the end of Rua do Chão da Feira leads through to Rua dos Cegos and down to Largo Rodrigues de Freitas, which marks the eastern edge of **Mouraria**, the district to which the Moors were relegated

THE SÉ, CASTELO AND ALFAMA

The Mouraria district

after the siege of Lisbon – hence the name. Today Mouraria is an atmospheric residential area.

Miradouro da Graça

MAP P.38, POCKET MAP F10

The **Miradouro da Graça** provides superb views over Lisbon and the castle. To reach it take tram #28 (see page 43) to the broad Largo da Graça. From here, head past Nossa Senhora da Graça – a church which partly dates from 1271, making it one of the oldest in the city – to the viewpoint which also has a small kiosk café-bar. Below the *miradouro*, steps lead down to the Jardim da Cerca da Graça, one of Lisbon's newest parks. There's a children's play area, lawns and appealing walkways.

Intendente

MAP P.38, POCKET MAP K5

Served by tram #28, the area of **Intendente** was recently down-at-heel and best avoided, certainly after dark, but is now an area to be seen. Its turnaround was driven by the opening of the superb Art Nouveau Lisboa Hotel 1908 (see page 127) on one side of its

pedestrianized square, and the hip Casa Independent (see page 48) cultural centre on the other. Now, the square and its surrounding streets are abuzz with cafés, bars and restaurants, many in beautiful, tile-fronted buildings. You can take the stepped alleys to the east of the square for a steep 15-minute walk up to Miradouro Senhora do Monte, Lisbon's highest point and a great look-out spot.

São Vicente de Fora

MAP P.38, POCKET MAP G11

Largo de São Vicente, Tram #28 ☎ 218 885 652, church free, charge for monastery.

The church of **São Vicente de Fora** stands as a reminder of the extent of the sixteenth-century city; its name means "Saint Vincent of the Outside". It was built during the years of Spanish rule by Philip II's Italian architect, Felipe Terzi (1582–1629); its geometric facade was an important Renaissance innovation. Of more interest is the adjoining monastery, home to the world's largest collection of Baroque tiles. Through the beautiful cloisters, decorated

Santa Engrácia

Tram #28

The picture-book tram #28 (6am–10.30pm, every 15min) is one of the city's greatest rides, though its popularity is such that there are usually queues to get on and standing-room-only is more than likely. Built in England in the early twentieth century, the trams are all polished wood and chrome, but give a distinctly rough ride up and down Lisbon's steepest streets, at times coming so close to shops that you could almost take a can of sardines off the shelves. From Graça, the tram plunges down through Alfama to the Baixa and up to Prazeres, to the west of the centre. Take care of belongings as pickpockets also enjoy the ride.

with *azulejos* representing scenes from Portugal's history, you can visit the old monastic refectory, which since 1855 has formed the pantheon of the Bragança dynasty. Here, in more or less complete sequence, are the **tombs** of all the Portuguese kings from João IV, who restored the monarchy in 1640, to Manuel II, the last Portuguese monarch who died in exile in England in 1932. Among them is Catherine of Bragança, the widow of England's Charles II, who is credited with introducing the concept of "teatime" to the British. If you have energy, climb to the roof for spectacular views out over the city. There's also a lovely café by the entrance if you do fancy a cup of tea.

Feira da Ladra

MAP P.38, POCKET MAP H10
Campo de Santa Clara, Tram #28.

The leafy square of Campo de Santa Clara is home to the twice-weekly **Feira da Ladra** ("Thieves' Market"), Lisbon's main flea market. It's not the world's greatest market, but it does turn up some interesting things, like oddities from the former African colonies and old Portuguese prints. Out-and-out junk – from broken alarm clocks to old postcards – is spread on the ground above Santa Engrácia, with cheap clothes, CDs and half-genuine antiques at the top end of the *feira*. The covered *mercado* (market) building

has a fine array of fresh fruit and vegetables.

Santa Engrácia

MAP P.38, POCKET MAP H10
Campo de Santa Clara, Tram #28
🌐 panteaonacional.gov.pt, charge.

The white dome of **Santa Engrácia** makes it the loftiest church in the city, and it has become synonymous with unfinished work – begun in 1682, it was only completed in 1966. It is now the **Panteão Nacional**, housing the tombs of eminent Portuguese figures, including writer Almeida Garrett (1799–1854) and Amália Rodrigues (1920–99), Portugal's most famous fado singer, and football legend Eusébio (1942–2014). You can take the stairs up to the terrace, from where there are great views over eastern Lisbon.

The Alfama

MAP P.38, POCKET MAP G12

In Moorish times, the **Alfama** was the grandest part of the city, but as Lisbon expanded, the new Christian nobility moved out, leaving it to the local fishing community. None of today's houses dates from before the Christian Reconquest, but you'll notice a kasbah-like layout. Although an increasing number of fado restaurants are moving in, the quarter retains a quiet, village-like quality. Life continues much as it has done for years with people buying groceries and fish from hole-in-the-wall stores and householders stoking small outdoor charcoal grills. Half the fun of exploring here is getting lost, but head for Rua de São Miguel – off which run some of the most interesting *becos* (alleys) – and for the parallel street Rua de São Pedro.

Igreja de Santo Estêvão

MAP P.38. POCKET MAP G11
Largo de Santo Estêvão, Tram #28 ☎ 213 912 600, free.

The handsome church of **Santo Estêvão** was built in 1733 and was partly damaged in the 1755 earthquake, leaving it with one of its two original towers. Its Baroque interior is impressive but is usually open only for Mass (Sunday at 10am). However, it's worth a visit if only to see the view over the river from its terrace.

Museu do Fado

MAP P.38, POCKET MAP G12
Largo do Chafariz de Dentro 1
Ⓦ museudofado.pt, charge.

Set in the renovated Recinto da Praia, a former water cistern and bathhouse, the **Museu do Fado** provides an excellent introduction

to this quintessentially Portuguese art form (see box, page 45). It also has a good restaurant. The museum details the history of fado and its importance to the Portuguese people; its shop stocks a great selection of CDs. A series of rooms in the museum contains wax models, photographs, famous paintings of fado scenes and descriptions of the leading singers. It also traces the history of the Portuguese guitar, an essential element of the fado performance. Interactive displays allow you to listen to the different types of fado (Lisbon has its own kind, differing from that of the northern city of Coimbra), varying from mournful to positively racy.

Barbadinhos Steam Pumping Station

MAP P.38, POCKET MAP M5
Rua do Alviela 12 Ⓦ epal.pt, charge.

Ten minutes' walk from Santa Apolónia metro, off Calçada dos Barbadinhos, the **Barbadinhos Steam Pumping Station** is a small but engaging museum housed in an attractive old pumping station filled with shiny brass, polished

Tram 28 in the Alfama

Fado

Fado (literally "fate") is often described as a kind of Portuguese blues. Popular themes are love, death, bullfighting and indeed fate itself. It is believed to derive from music that was popular with eighteenth-century immigrants from Portugal's colonies who first settled in Alfama. Famous singers like Maria Severa and Amália Rodrigues grew up in Alfama, which since the 1930s has hosted some of the city's most authentic fado houses – stroll around after 8pm and you'll hear magical sounds emanating from various venues, or better still, enjoy a meal at one of the places listed on page 46. The big contemporary names are Ana Moura, Mariza, who grew up in neighbouring Mouraria, and Cuca Roseta. Other singers to look out for (though unlikely to appear in small venues) are Mísia, Carminho, Helder Moutinho, Carlos do Carmo, Maria da Fé, Raquel Tavares, Camané and Cristina Branco.

wood and Victorian ingenuity. It was built in 1880 to pump water from a nearby river up Lisbon's steep hills, depositing it in a reservoir hollowed out from a former Franciscan convent. It used four steam-powered engines that worked nonstop until 1928 and which you can see demonstrated today. The museum is the main branch of Lisbon's Museu da Água (water museum; see page 62), and its exhibits give a fascinating insight into the evolution of the city's water supply.

Museu Nacional do Azulejo

MAP P.38, POCKET MAP M5
Rua da Madre de Deus 4. Bus #794 from Praça do Comércio/Santa Apolónia
🌐 museudoazulejo.pt, charge.

The **Museu Nacional do Azulejo** (tile museum) traces the development of Portuguese *azulejo* tiles from fifteenth-century Moorish styles to the present day, with each room representing a different period. Diverse styles range from seventeenth-century portraits of the English King Charles II with his Portuguese wife, Catherine of Bragança, to the 1720 satirical panel depicting a man being given an injection in his bottom. The museum is inside the church Madre de Deus, whose eighteenth-century tiled scenes of St Anthony are among the best in the city. Many of the rooms are housed round the church's cloisters – look for the spire in one corner of the main cloister, itself completely tiled. The highlight upstairs is Portugal's longest *azulejo* – a wonderfully detailed 40-metre panorama of Lisbon, completed in around 1738. The museum also has a good café-restaurant and shop.

Patio of the Museu Nacional do Azulejo

Shop

Conserveira de Lisboa

MAP P.38, POCKET MAP E13
Rua dos Bacalhoeiras 34.
Wall-to-wall tin cans stuffed into wooden cabinets make this colourful 1930s shop a bizarre but intriguing place to stock up on tinned sardines, squid, salmon, mussels and just about any other sea beast you can think of.

Restaurants

A Mourisca

MAP P.38, POCKET MAP F10
Largo da Graça 84–85 ☎ 218 863 688.
Bustling *cervejaria* whose draping of soccer scarves doesn't quite hide the beautifully tiled walls. There's a sizzling good range of fish and meat here, including pork steaks, squid kebabs and *arroz de marisco* (seafood rice dish), which is good value for two people. €€

Conserveira de Lisboa

Arco do Castelo

MAP P.38, POCKET MAP F12
Rua do Chão da Feira 25 ☎ 218 876 598.
Cheerful, long-established Indian just below the entrance to the castle, specializing in moderately priced Goan dishes – there's a fine shrimp curry, and *feijoada indiana* (spicy bean stew). €€

Barracão de Alfama

MAP P.38, POCKET MAP G12
Rua de S. Pedro 16 ☎ 218 866 359.
An unpretentious local *tasca* popular with locals, with non-touristy prices: there are outdoor tables in summer. Portions are generous with fine fish and grilled meats. €€

Casanova

MAP P.38, POCKET MAP M6
Avda Infante Dom Henrique, Loja 7
Armazém B, Cais da Pedra à Bica do Sapato
Ⓦ pizzeriacasanova.pt.
Very popular Italian serving pizza, pasta and *crostini* with sumptuous river views from its terrace (when

Eggs at Santa Clara dos Cogumelos

the cruise ships aren't blocking the view). You can't book, so turn up early. €€

Cervejaria Ramiro

MAP P.38, POCKET MAP K5
Avenida Almirante Reis 1
Ⓦ cervejariaramiro.pt.
Fabulous, famous and extremely popular fish restaurant whose decor has changed little since it opened in 1956. It's set across three floors; the basement is full of bubbling fish tanks, while the ground floor is usually rammed with clients downing its famed garlic prawns, lobster, crab and the like. Live soccer is likely to be on TV. Queue for a table. €€

Estrela da Sé

MAP P.38, POCKET MAP E12
Largo S. António da Sé 4 Ⓣ 218 870 455.
Beautiful *azulejo*-covered restaurant near the Sé, serving inexpensive and tasty dishes like *alheira* (chicken sausage), salmon and Spanish-style tapas. Its wooden booths – perfect for discreet trysts – date from the nineteenth century. €€

Infame

MAP P.26, POCKET MAP H8
Largo do Intendente Pina Manique 4
Ⓦ infame.pt.
Inside the classy Hotel Lisboa 1908, this is an Art Nouveau gem with a galleried interior. The menu is influenced by Portugal's former colonies, so expect dishes such as oyster gyozo, cod *piri piri* or octopus with sweet potato and pak choi. Don't miss a drink in the adjacent bar. €€€

Pateo 13

MAP P.38, POCKET MAP G12
Calcadinha de Santo Estevão 13 Ⓣ 210 503 434.
Apart from the kitchen, this is formed entirely of outdoor seating – so opening is weather-dependent. But for most of the year, the charming patio is the perfect spot for excellent value grilled fish, including seabass and sardines. The house wine is very affordable. €

Santa Clara dos Cogumelos

MAP P.38, POCKET MAP H10
Mercado de Santa Clara 7
Ⓦ santaclaradoscogumelos.com.
In a lovely room above the market building, this very good Italian-run restaurant specializes in mushroom-themed dishes. Try the mushroom risotto, gnocchi, salmon with mushroom sauce, or the porcini ice cream. €€

Clube de Fado

Via Graça

MAP P.38, POCKET MAP K5
Rua Damasceno Monteiro 9b
Ⓦ restauranteviagraca.com.
Near the Miradouro da Graça,
this sophisticated and highly
rated restaurant in an unattractive
modern building is better on the
inside, from where you can enjoy
the stunning panorama. Specialities
include roast goat, game and
bacalhau dishes. €€€€

Café

Largo Café

MAP P.38, POCKET MAP K5
Largo do Intendente Pina Manique 19
Ⓣ 218 879 401.
This café sits below an artists'
residency and its sunny outdoor
tables on the square attract an arty
crowd. Check out the counter for
the daily specials – many of them
vegetarian – and it also serves
inexpensive drinks, including shots
and cocktails. €

Bars and clubs

Casa Independente

MAP P.38, POCKET MAP K5
Largo do Intendente Pina Manique 45
Ⓦ casaindependente.com.
Unassuming from the outside,
this wonderful rambling building
is credited with kick-starting
Independente's cool credentials.
Part club, part music venue and
part cultural centre, it consists
of various rooms where you can
admire works of art, listen to surf
rock or Zouk bass (check the
website for what's on) or simply
chat over a drink. Great terrace.

Chapitô

MAP P.38, POCKET MAP E12
Costa do Castelo 7 Ⓦ www.chapito.org.
Multipurpose venue incorporating
a theatre, circus school, restaurant
and tapas bar. The restaurant,
Chapitô à Mesa, is in an upstairs
dining room, reached via a spiral
staircase, and serves mains such

as black pork with ginger and mushroom risotto. The outdoor esplanade commands terrific views over Alfama and most people come here to drink and take in the view; reservations advised. Check the website for live music, films and readings.

Lux

MAP P.38, POCKET MAP M6
Armazém A, Cais de Pedra a Santa Apolónia ⓦ luxfragil.com.

This converted former meat warehouse is one of Europe's most fashionable spaces, attracting A-list visitors such as Cameron Diaz. Part-owned by actor John Malkovich, it was the first place to venture into the docks opposite Santa Apolónia station. There's a rooftop terrace with amazing views, various bars, projection screens, a frenzied downstairs dancefloor, and music from pop and trance to jazz and dance. The club is also on the circuit for touring bands.

Portas do Sol

MAP P.38, POCKET MAP G12
Largo Portas do Sol ⓦ www.portasdosol.pt.

As you might guess from the name, this hip spot is an obligatory venue for anyone into sunsets. Hiding under the lip of the road, it's a chic indoor space, though most people head for the outside seats on the giant terrace with grandstand views over the Alfama. Pricey drinks, coffees and cocktails, but worth it. DJs on Fridays and Saturdays.

Fado and music venues

A Baiuca

MAP P.38, POCKET MAP G12
Rua de São Miguel 20 ☎ 218 867 284.

Nightly *fado vadio* ("casual" fado) is performed in this great little tiled *tasca*, which serves decent fresh fish and grills; minimum spend is €25. Reservations advised.

A Parreirinha de Alfama

MAP P.38, POCKET MAP G12
Beco do Espírito Santo 1
ⓦ parreirinhadealfama.com.

One of the best fado venues owned by famous fado singer Argentina Santos, just off Largo do Chafariz de Dentro, often attracting leading stars and an enthusiastic local clientele. Reservations are advised when the big names appear.

Clube de Fado

MAP P.38, POCKET MAP F12
Rua de São João da Praça 86–94 ⓦ clube-de-fado.com.

Intimate fado club with stone pillars, an old well as a decorative feature, and a mainly local clientele. It attracts small-time performers, up-and-coming talent and the occasional big name. Expect to pay €60 (including food).

Mesa de Frades

MAP P.38, POCKET MAP L7
Rua dos Remédios 139a ☎ 917 029 436.

Set in a beautiful former chapel and richly adorned with decorative tiles, this intimate space was in the spotlight in 2018 when Madonna popped in for an impromptu singalong. Less illustrious performers are usually just as engaging.

Entrance to Chapitô

Chiado and Cais do Sodré

The well-to-do district of Chiado (pronounced she-ar-doo) is famed for its smart shops and cafés, along with the city's main museum for contemporary arts. Down on the waterfront, Cais do Sodré (kaiysh-doo-soodray) is one of the city's "in" districts. Many of its waterfront warehouses have been converted into upmarket cafés and restaurants and by day, in particular, a stroll along its characterful riverfront is very enjoyable. Nearby Lisbon's main market, Mercado da Ribeira, aka Time Out Market, is also big on atmosphere, as is the hillside Bica district, which is served by another of the city's classic funicular street lifts – Elevador da Bica. Cais do Sodré is also where you can catch ferries across the Tejo to the little port of Cacilhas, which not only has some great seafood restaurants with views over Lisbon, but is also the bus terminus for some of the region's best beaches and for the spectacular Cristo Rei statue of Christ.

Rua Garrett

MAP P.52, POCKET MAP C12

Chiado's most famous street, **Rua Garrett**, is where you'll find some of the oldest shops and cafés in the city, including *A Brasileira* (see page 56). Beggars usually mark the nearby entrance to the **Igreja dos Mártires** (Church of the Martyrs), named after the English Crusaders who were killed during the siege of Lisbon. Some of the area's best shops can also be found in nearby Rua do Carmo. This was the heart of the area that was greatly damaged by a fire in 1988, although the original belle époque atmosphere has since been superbly re-created under the direction of eminent Portuguese architect Álvaro Siza Vieira.

Museu Nacional de Arte Contemporânea do Chiado

MAP P.52, POCKET MAP C13
Rua Serpa Pinto 4 Ⓜ museuarte
contemporanea.gov.pt, charge.

The **National Museum of Contemporary Art** traces the history of art from Romanticism to Modernism. It is housed in a stylish building with a pleasant courtyard café and rooftop terrace, constructed around a nineteenth-century biscuit factory. Within the gallery's permanent collection are works by some of Portugal's most influential artists since the nineteenth century, along with foreign artists influenced by Portugal including Rodin. Highlights include Almada Negreiros' 1920s panels from the old São Carlos cinema, showing Felix the Cat; a beautiful sculpture, *A Viúva* (The Widow), by António Teixeira Lopes; and some evocative early twentieth-century Lisbon scenes by watercolourist Carlos Botelho. There are also frequent temporary exhibitions.

Elevador da Bica

MAP P.52, POCKET MAP B13
Entrance on Rua de São Paulo, charge.

With its entrance tucked into an arch on Rua de São Paulo, the **Elevador da Bica** is one of the city's most atmospheric

Tram #25 to Prazeres

You can catch another of Lisbon's classic tram rides, the #25, from Praça da Figueira (Mon–Fri 6.30am–8.30pm, every 15min). This sees far fewer tourists than tram #28 (see page 43), but takes almost as picturesque a route. From here it trundles along the riverfront and up through Lapa and Estrela to the suburb of Prazeres, best known as the site of one of Lisbon's largest cemeteries. You can stroll round the enormous plot where family tombs are movingly adorned with trinkets and photos of the deceased.

funicular railways. Built in 1892 – and originally powered by water counterweights, but now electrically operated – the *elevador* leads up towards the Bairro Alto, via a steep residential street. Take time to explore the steep side-streets of the Bica neighbourhood too, a warren of characterful houses, little shops and fine local restaurants.

Mercado da Ribeira/Time Out Market

MAP P.52, POCKET MAP B13
Main entrance on Avda 24 de Julho
ⓦ timeoutmarket.com/lisboa. Fruit, fish and vegetable market Mon–Sat 6am–2pm; food stalls daily 10am–midnight.

Built originally on the site of an old fort at the end of the nineteenth century, the **Mercado da Ribeira** is Lisbon's most historic market, though most of the current structure dates only from 1930. Inside, stalls sell an impressive array of fresh fish, fruit and vegetables, with a separate, aromatic flower section. However, much of the building is now given over to the vibrant Time Out Market, filled with an impressive range of food stalls and plenty of communal benches; it's a great place to sample dishes from some of the city's top chefs, such as Vincent Farges and Henrique Sá Pessoa, or you can choose something simple like a

Mercado da Ribeira

Chiado and Cais do Sodré

Travel to Cacilhas and beyond

Cais do Sodré is the main departure point for ferries over the Tejo to the largely industrial suburbs to the south. Ferries to Cacilhas (ⓦ transtejo.pt, 5.35am–1.40am, last return 1.20am, every 15–20min, charge) dock by a bus and tram depot from where buses run to Costa da Caparica (see page 121).

prego (steak sandwich) or pizza. You pay slightly above the norm for the concept and ambience, but with everything from hams, cheeses and grilled chicken to gourmet burgers, seafood, organic salads and chocolates (not to mention champagne and cocktail bars), you might well find yourself tempted back here again and again. On Sunday mornings there's a collectors' market, while additional outlets line up around the outside of the market building.

Rua Cor-de-Rosa

MAP P.52, POCKET MAP C13

Rua Nova do Carvalho's once dodgy clubs and bars have now (largely) been revamped into some of the city's coolest hangouts. The rebranding has extended to the colour of the street, which is now pink, hence the nickname **Rua Cor-de-Rosa** (Pink Street). We list some of the best places on page 56.

Cacilhas and Almada

MAP P.52, POCKET MAP J8

The short, blustery ferry ride from Lisbon's Cais do Sodré over the Tejo to Cacilhas is great fun and grants wonderful views of the city. **Cacilhas** is little more than a somewhat rundown bus, tram and ferry terminal with a pretty church, surrounded by lively stalls and cafés, but is well known for its seafood restaurants. You can also visit the wooden-hulled, fifty-gun **Dom Fernando II e Glória frigate** (ⓦ ccm.marinha.pt, charge) on Largo Alfredo Diniz. Built in India in 1843, it's now a museum showing what life at sea was like in the mid-nineteenth century.

A good riverside walk is to head west towards the bridge along the waterfront. It's around fifteen minutes' walk to the **Elevador Panorâmico da Boca do Vento** (daily 10am–9pm, charge), a sleek lift that whisks you 30m up the cliff face to the attractive old part of **Almada**, giving fantastic views.

Cristo Rei

MAP P.52, POCKET MAP H9

Bus #101 from outside the Cacilhas ferry terminal ⓦ cristorei.pt, charge for lift.

On the heights above Almada stand the outstretched arms of **Cristo Rei** (Christ the King). Inspired by Rio's famous *Cristo Redentor* statue, it was built in 1959 as a pilgrimage site to grace Portugal's non-participation in World War II. A lift shuttles you 80m up the plinth, where a few stairs lead to a dramatic viewing platform at the foot of the statue, from which, on a clear day, you can catch a glimpse of the glistening roof of the Pena palace at Sintra.

Cristo Rei

Shops

A Vida Portuguesa

MAP P.52, POCKET MAP C12
Rua Anchieta 11.

An expensive but evocative collection of retro toys, crafts and ceramics, beautifully displayed and packaged in a historic former perfumery.

Armazéns do Chiado

MAP P.52, POCKET MAP D12
Rua do Carmo 2.

This swish shopping centre sits on six floors above metro Baixa-Chiado in a structure that has risen from the ashes of the Chiado fire, though it retains its traditional facade. Various shops include branches of Pepe Jeans, Fnac, The Body Shop and Mango. The top floor has a series of cafés and restaurants, most offering great views.

Fábrica Sant'Anna

MAP P.52, POCKET MAP C13
Largo Barão de Quintela, 4, off Rua do Alecrim. Ⓦ santanna.com.

A great place to find out more about Portuguese *azulejos*, and to buy a few souvenirs to take home. Founded in 1741, the factory shop still makes ceramics on the premises using traditional techniques and sells a wide range of handmade ceramics, plus copies of classic designs.

Livraria Bertrand

MAP P.52, POCKET MAP C12
Rua Garrett 73.

Officially the world's oldest bookshop, founded in 1732 and once the meeting place for Lisbon's literary set. Offering novels in English and a range of foreign magazines, it's also a good place to find English translations of Portuguese writers, including Fernando Pessoa.

Luvaria Ulisses

MAP P.52, POCKET MAP D11
Rua do Carmo 87a.

The superb, ornately carved wooden doorway leads you into a minuscule glove shop, with hand-wear to suit all tastes tucked into rows of boxes.

Storytailors

Manteigaria

MAP P.52, POCKET MAP B12
Rua do Loreto 2.

This tiny shop specializes in *pastéis de nata*, those delectable custard tarts, served piping hot and some say the best in the city. It also serves coffee and, somewhat bizarrely, port.

Storytailors

MAP P.52, POCKET MAP C13
Calçada do Ferragial 8.

Set in a suitably stylish, bare-brick eighteenth-century former warehouse, the shop interior is as magical as its designer clothes inspired by fairy tales. Its haute couture range has been snapped up by the likes of Madonna and Lily Allen, though you'll need a rock star's salary to afford it.

Restaurants

Cantinho do Avillez

MAP P.52, POCKET MAP C13
Rua dos Duques de Bragança 7
Ⓦ cantinhodoavillez.pt.

In a contemporary space, with tram #28 rattling by its door, this laid-back but classy canteen is a good place to sample food from Lisbon's top chef, José Avillez, at reasonable prices. Delectable mains include the likes of sauteed scallops with mushroom risotto, or Alentejo pork with coriander. Starters include a superb baked Nisa cheese, and the house wines are equally top-notch. €€€

Cervejaria Farol

MAP P.52, POCKET MAP H9
Largo Alfredo Dinis 1–3, Cacilhas
Ⓦ restaurantefarol.com.

The most high-profile seafood restaurant in Cacilhas, with fine views across the Tejo to match. If you feel extravagant, it's hard to beat the lobsters, though other fish and meat dishes are better value. *Azulejos* on the wall show the old *farol* (lighthouse) that once stood

here – the restaurant is located along the quayside, on the right as you leave the ferry. €€

Ibo

MAP P.52, POCKET MAP H8
Armazén A, Compartimento 2, Cais do Sodré. Ⓦ ibo-restaurant.pt.

Named after an island off the north coast of Mozambique and set in an old salt warehouse, this classy restaurant serves delicious dishes from Portugal's former colony, such as octopus *açorda* and aubergine gratin, with a wonderful riverside terrace. There is also a less expensive next-door café-bar, where you can pop in for a drink or snack. €€

La Brasserie L'Entrecôte

MAP P.52, POCKET MAP C12
Rua do Alecrim 117–120
Ⓦ brasserieentrecote.pt.

This upmarket restaurant has won awards for its entrecôte steak, which is just as well, as that's all it serves (though there is a vegetarian steak too). With a sauce said to contain 35 ingredients, it is truly delicious. Reservations advised. €€€

Pap-Açorda

MAP P.52, POCKET MAP B14
Primeiro Piso do Mercado da Ribeira
Ⓦ papacorda.com.

Pap-Açorda was the place to be seen when it was in the Bairro Alto, and though it's not quite as fashionable as it was, the famous old restaurant now boats a classy first-floor position above Time Out Market with fine views over the square. It specializes in *açorda* dishes, served with a garlicky bread sauce. Try the *açorda de gambas* (with prawns) or the fantastic John Dory filets. €€€

Rio Grande

MAP P.52, POCKET MAP B12
Rua Nova do Carvalho 55 ☏ 213 423 804.

It might be on a street full of hip bars, but *Rio Grande* is reassuringly traditional, with *azulejos* on the walls beneath a vaulted ceiling. The spacious restaurant serves up good-value Portuguese classics such as pork steaks and a good array of fresh fish. €€

Vicente

MAP P.52, POCKET MAP C13
Rua das Flores 6 ☎ 936 725 384.
Fashionable café-restaurant with a brick-vaulted ceiling and seats outside on a small square. Specialities are meaty dishes from the Alentejo, the region between Lisbon and the Algarve: the steaks and sausages are wonderful, as are its range of *petiscos*, tapas-like snacks. €€

Cafés

Benard

MAP P.52, POCKET MAP C12
Rua Garrett 104.
Often overlooked because of its proximity to *A Brasileira*, this ornate nineteenth-century café

Café a Brasileira

offers superb cakes, croissants and *pastéis de nata*; it also has a hugely popular outdoor terrace on Chiado's most fashionable street. €

Café a Brasileira

MAP P.52, POCKET MAP C12
Rua Garrett 122.
Opened in 1905, and marked by an outdoor bronze statue of the poet Fernando Pessoa, this is the most famous of Lisbon's old-style coffee houses. The tables on the pedestrianized street get snapped up by tourists but the real appeal is in its traditional interior, where prices are considerably cheaper, especially if you stand at the long bar. At night, buskers often add a frisson as the clientele changes to a more youthful brigade, all on the beer. €€

Leitaria Académica

MAP P.52, POCKET MAP C12
Largo do Carmo 1–3.
Outdoor tables on one of the city's leafiest squares. Besides drinks and snacks, it also does light lunches; the tasty grilled sardines are perfect in summer. €

Bars and clubs

A Tabacaria

MAP P.52, POCKET MAP B13
Rua de São Paulo 75–77 ☎ 213 420 281.
In a wonderful old tobacco shop dating back to 1885 – with many of the original fittings – this cosy bar specializes in cocktails made from gin, vodka, whisky and seasonal fruits.

Music Box

MAP P.52, POCKET MAP C13
Rua Nova do Carvalho 24
Ⓦ musicboxlisboa.com.
Tucked under the arches of Rua Nova do Carvalho is this cool cultural and music venue which hosts club nights, live music, films and performing arts, with an emphasis on promoting

Palácio Chiado

independent acts. There's a top sound and light system and usually a buzzy, happy crowd.

Palácio Chiado

MAP P.52. POCKET MAP C12
Rua do Alecrim 70 Ⓦ palaciochiado.pt.
This ornate former eighteenth-century palace has been transformed into a hip outlet for various bars and restaurants. Head to the top floor for a stunning bar area, complete with a golden-winged lion suspended overhead, for a range of tantalising cocktails including O Mistério, a cherry liqueur with lime and basil. The adjacent room has good views over Chiado.

Pensão Amor

MAP P.52, POCKET MAP C13
Rua Nova do Carvalho, 38 Ⓣ 213 143 399.
The "Pension of Love" is a former "house of ill-repute" that now serves tasty cocktails. It has retained its eighteenth-century burlesque fittings for its current incarnation as a trendy bar with risqué photos,

frescoes and mirrors. You can browse through the small erotic bookstore or enjoy occasional live concerts.

Povo

MAP P.52, POCKET MAP C13
Rua Nova do Carvalho 32–26
Ⓦ povolisboa.com.
This fashionable tavern in the heart of "Pink Street" offers fado from up-and-coming stars and late-night DJs at weekends, plus Monday poetry readings. There's a great menu of *petiscos* and mains such as mussels with seaweed, *bacalhau* dishes and steaks.

Sol e Pesca

MAP P.52, POCKET MAP C13
Rua Nova do Carvalho 44 Ⓣ 213 467 203.
Once a shop selling fishing equipment, this is now a hip bar. The fishing equipment is part of the decor, and you can still purchase tinned fish to enjoy with bread and wine at low stools inside, or outside on trendy "Pink Street".

Bairro Alto and São Bento

The Bairro Alto, the Upper Town, sits on a hill west of the Baixa. After the 1755 earthquake, the relatively unscathed district became the favoured haunt of Lisbon's young bohemians. Home to the Institute of Art and Design and various designer boutiques, it is still the city's most fashionable district. By day, the central grid of narrow, cobbled streets feels residential. After dark, however, the area throngs with people visiting its famed fado houses, bars and restaurants, while the city's LGBTQ community coalesces around the clubs of neighbouring Príncipe Real. There are impressive monuments too, including the Palácio da Assembléia, Portugal's parliamentary building in nearby São Bento. This area houses good ethnic restaurants, a legacy of the city's first black community established by the descendants of African slaves.

Elevador da Glória

MAP P.60, POCKET MAP C11

Everyone should ride the **Elevador da Glória** at least once. From the bottom of Calçada da Glória (off Praça dos Restauradores, see page 30), the funicular climbs the knee-jarringly sheer street in

Elevador da Glória

a couple of minutes, leaving the lower city behind as you ascend above its rooftops. An amazing feat of engineering, the tram system was built in 1885. It was originally powered by water displacement, later replaced by steam, and now runs on electricity.

At the top, pause at the gardens, the **Miradouro de São Pedro de Alcântara**, from where there's a superb view across the city to the castle.

Igreja de São Roque

MAP P.60, POCKET MAP C11
Largo de Trindade Coelha
Ⓦ museusaoroque.scml.pt, free.

The sixteenth-century **Igreja de São Roque** looks like the plainest church in the city, with its bleak Renaissance facade. Yet inside lies an astonishing succession of lavishly decorated side chapels. The highlight is the **Capela de São João Baptista**, for its size the most expensive chapel ever constructed. It was ordered from Rome in 1742 by Dom João V to honour his patron saint and, more dubiously, to gratify Pope

Benedict XIV whom he had persuaded to confer a patriarchate on Lisbon. It was erected at the Vatican for the Pope to celebrate Mass in, before being dismantled and shipped to Lisbon at the then vast cost of €300,000. If you examine the four "oil paintings" of John the Baptist's life, you'll find that they are in fact intricately worked mosaics. The more valuable parts of the altar front are kept in the adjacent **museum** (charge), which also displays sixteenth- to eighteenth-century paintings and a motley collection of church relics.

Convento do Carmo

MAP P.60, POCKET MAP D12
Largo do Carmo
Ⓦ museuarqueologicodocarmo.pt, charge.

Built between 1389 and 1423, and once the largest church in the city, the **Convento do Carmo** was partially destroyed by the 1755 earthquake, but is even more striking as a result, with its beautiful Gothic arches rising grandly into the sky. Today it houses the splendid **Museu Arqueológico do Carmo**, home to many of the treasures from monasteries that were dissolved after the 1834 revolution. The entire nave is open to the elements, with columns and statuary scattered in all corners. Inside, on either side of what was the main altar, are the main exhibits, centering on a series of tombs. Largest is the beautifully carved, stone tomb of Ferdinand I; nearby, that of Gonçalo de Sousa, chancellor to Henry the Navigator, is topped by a statue of Gonçalo himself. There is also an Egyptian sarcophagus, whose inhabitant's feet are just visible underneath the lid; and, equally alarmingly, two pre-Columbian mummies which lie in glass cases, alongside the preserved heads of a couple of Peruvian Indians.

The exit to the **Elevador de Santa Justa** (see page 29) is at

Convento do Carmo

the side of the Convento do Carmo – go onto the rampway leading to it for fine views over the city or the partly lawned terrace in front, the **Terraços do Carmo**, with its handy café.

Bairro Alto

MAP P.60, POCKET MAP B11

Quiet by day, the graffitied central streets of the **Bairro Alto** buzz with people after dark, especially on summer weekends when the streets become a giant mass of partygoers. The liveliest area is the tight network of streets to the west of Rua da Misericórdia, particularly after midnight in Rua do Norte, Rua Diário de Notícias, Rua da Atalaia and Rua da Rosa. Running steeply downhill, Rua do Século is one of the area's most historic streets. A sign at no. 89 marks the birthplace of the Marquês de Pombal, the minister responsible for rebuilding Lisbon after the Great Earthquake.

Miradouro de Santa Catarina

MAP P.60, POCKET MAP A12
Tram #28.

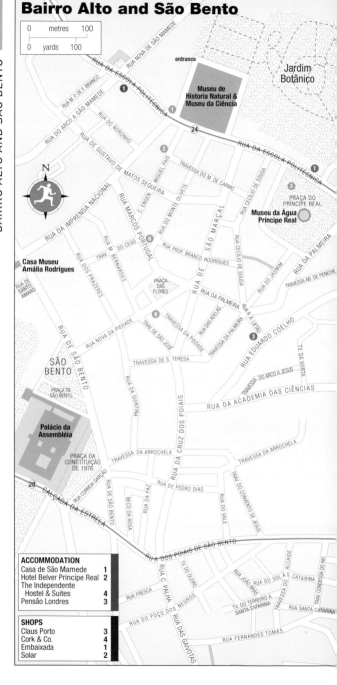

Bairro Alto and São Bento

0 metres 100
0 yards 100

entrance

Jardim Botânico

Museu de Historia Natural & Museu da Ciência

RUA NOVA DE SÃO MAMEDE

RUA DA ESCOLA POLITÉCNICA

RUA M. P. DE F. BRANCO

RUA DO ARCO A SÃO MAMEDE

RUA DO NORONHO

RUA DE GUSTAVO DE MATOS SEQUEIRA

RUA MIGUEL PAIS

TRAVESSA DO M. DE CARMO

24

RUA DA ESCOLA POLITÉCNICA

RUA CECÍLIO DE SOUSA

PRAÇA DO PRÍNCIPE REAL

Museu da Água Príncipe Real

RUA DA PALMEIRA

N

RUA DA IMPRENSA NACIONAL

RUA MARCOS PORTUGAL

RUA C. EUGEN

RUA DO MONTE OLIVETE

RUA DE SÃO MARÇAL

RUA CECÍLIO DE SOUSA

RUA DO JASMIM

TRAVESSA AB. DE PENICHE

Casa Museu Amália Rodrigues

RUA DE SANTO AMARO

RUA DOS PRAZERES

TRAV. M. BERNARDES

RUA DO CEGO

RUA PROF. BRANCO RODRIGUES

PRAÇA DAS FLORES

RUA DE SÃO MARÇAL

RUA DA PALMEIRA

RUA DAS ADELAS

RUA DA PALMEIRA

RUA A. LENO

TRAVESSA DA PALMEIRA

RUA EDUARDO COELHO

TV. DA HORTA

RUA NOVA DA PIEDADE

TRAV. DE SÃO JOSÉ

TRAVESSA DA PIEDADE

TRAVESSA DE S. TERESA

SÃO BENTO

RUA DE SÃO BENTO

PRAÇA DE SÃO BENTO

RUA DA QUINTINA

RUA DA CRUZ DOS POIAIS

TRAVESSA DO ARCO À JESUS

RUA DA ACADEMIA DAS CIÊNCIAS

Palácio da Assembléia

PRAÇA DA CONSTITUIÇÃO DE 1976

TRAVESSA DA ARROCHELA

TRAVESSA DA ARROCHELA

TRAV. DO CONVENTO DE JESUS

28

CALÇADA DA ESTRELA

RUA CORREIA GARÇÃO

RUA DE SÃO BENTO

BECO DA ROSA

RUA DA PAZ

TRAVESSA DA ARROCHELA

RUA DE PEDRO DIAS

RUA DO VALE

RUA DOS POIAIS DE SÃO BENTO

RUA C. PALHA

RUA DO OLEIRO

RUA FRESCA

RUA DO POÇO DOS NEGROS

RUA DAS GAIVOTAS

TV. DO TERREIRO À SANTA CATARINA

RUA JOÃO BRÁS

RUA DO SOL À S. CATARINA

TRAVESSA DO A. CATARINA

TRAV. CONFESSA DO RIO

RUA SANTA CATARINA

RUA FERNANDES TOMÁS

ACCOMMODATION

Casa de São Mamede	1
Hotel Belver Príncipe Real	2
The Independente Hostel & Suites	4
Pensão Londres	3

SHOPS

Claus Porto	3
Cork & Co.	4
Embaixada	1
Solar	2

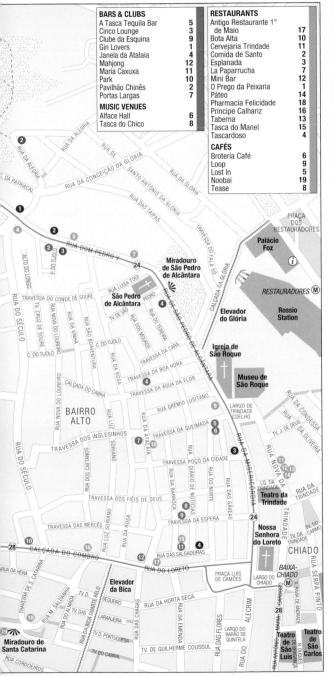

BARS & CLUBS

A Tasca Tequila Bar	5
Cinco Lounge	3
Clube da Esquina	9
Gin Lovers	1
Janela da Atalaia	4
Mahjong	12
Maria Caxuxa	11
Park	10
Pavilhão Chinês	2
Portas Largas	7

MUSIC VENUES

Alface Hall	6
Tasca do Chico	8

RESTAURANTS

Antigo Restaurante 1° de Maio	17
Bota Alta	10
Cervejaria Trindade	11
Comida de Santo	2
Esplanada	3
La Paparrucha	7
Mini Bar	12
O Prego da Peixaria	1
Páteo	14
Pharmacia Felicidade	18
Príncipe Calhariz	16
Taberna	13
Tasca do Manel	15
Tascardoso	4

CAFÉS

Broteria Café	6
Loop	9
Lost In	5
Noobai	19
Tease	8

At the bottom end of the Bairro Alto grid, set on the cusp of a hill high above the river, the railed **Miradouro de Santa Catarina** has spectacular views. Here, in the shadow of the statue of the Adamastor – a mythical beast from Luís de Camões's *Lusiads* – a mixture of oddballs and New Age types often collects around an alluring drinks kiosk, built in 1883, which has a few outdoor tables.

Praça do Príncipe Real

MAP P.60, POCKET MAP A10
Bus #758 from Chiado.
North of the Bairro Alto, the streets open out around the leafy **Praça do Príncipe Real**, one of the city's loveliest squares. Laid out in 1860 and surrounded by the ornate homes of former aristocrats – now mostly shops or offices – the square is the focal point of Lisbon's LGBTQ scene, though by day it is largely populated by families or locals playing cards under the trees.

Museu da Água Príncipe Real

MAP P.60, POCKET MAP A10
Praça do Príncipe Real 1. Bus #758 from Chiado ⓦ bit.ly/MuseuAgua, charge.
The **Museu da Água Príncipe Real** is accessed down steps in the centre of the square of the same name. Inside is an eerie nineteenth-century reservoir, where you can admire brick and vaulted ceilings, part of a network of tunnels that links up with the Aqueduto das Águas Livres (see page 94). Not for claustrophobics, the tours (book in advance) take you along one of these, a humid 410m tunnel that exits at the viewpoint of Miradouro de São Pedro (see page 58).

Museu Nacional de História e da Ciência

MAP P.60, POCKET MAP H5
Rua Escola Politécnica 56. Bus #758 from Chiado ⓦ museus.ulisboa.pt, charge (combined ticket includes entry to Jardim Botânico).
The nineteenth-century Neoclassical former technical college now hosts the mildly engaging museums of natural history known as the Museus de Politécnica. The **Museu da Ciência** (whose labs featured in the film *The Promise*, starring Christian Bale) has some absorbing geological

Lisbon graffiti

Graffiti has long been a feature of Lisbon life – in the form of political protest under the Salazar regime – and the council's heritage department has given over certain city walls to be part of a Galeria de Arte Urbana, in which street art is encouraged. The annual urban art festival, O Bairro i o Mundo, has been credited with alleviating some of the problems of the Quinta do Mocho district north of the airport. The result is a dazzling array of graffiti all over the city, but particularly around the Bairro Alto and the Alcântara docks. Lisbon's best-known graffiti artist is Alexandre Farto, aka Vhils, whose large and striking works are often chiselled into brickwork using pneumatic drills.

exhibits and a low-tech interactive section where you can balance balls on jets of air and swing pendulums among throngs of school kids.

The **Museu da História Natural** houses a rather dreary collection of stuffed animals, eggs and shells, though temporary exhibitions can be more diverting.

Jardim Botânico

MAP P.60, POCKET MAP H5
Rua Escola Politécnica 58 Ⓦ museus.
ulisboa.pt, charge (combined ticket includes Museu Nacional de História e da Ciência).

The lush **botanical gardens** are almost invisible from the surrounding streets and provide a tranquil escape from the city bustle. Portuguese explorers introduced many plant species to Europe during the golden age of exploration and these gardens, laid out between 1858 and 1878, are packed with twenty thousand neatly labelled species from around the world. Shady paths lead downhill under towering palms and luxuriant shrubs past a "Lugartagis" greenhouse for breeding butterflies.

Palácio da Assembléia

MAP P.60, POCKET MAP H6
Rua de São Bento. Tram #28.
Below the Bairro Alto in the district of São Bento, you can't miss the late sixteenth-century Neoclassical facade of the **Palácio da Assembléia**. Formerly a Benedictine monastery, it was taken over by the government in 1834 and today houses the Assembléia da República, Portugal's **parliament**. Since it's not open to the public (you can do an online tour on the website Ⓦ parlamento.pt), most visitors make do with the view of its steep white steps from tram #28 as it rattles along Calçada da Estrela, though it is worth exploring the earthy streets nearby. This was where Lisbon's black community put down roots – Rua do Poço dos Negros (Black Man's Well) takes its awful name from the corpses of slaves tossed into a hole here.

Casa Museu Amália Rodrigues

MAP P.60, POCKET MAP G6
Rua de São Bento 193, bus #706 from Cais do Sodré, or a short walk from tram #28 Ⓦ amaliarodrigues.pt, charge.

The daughter of an Alfama orange-seller, **Amália Rodrigues** was the undisputed queen of fado music until her death in 1999. The house where she lived since the 1950s has been kept as it was, and you can also admire original posters advertising her performances on stage and in the cinema, portraits by Portuguese artists and some of her personal possessions, and there are also live fado sessions on Saturdays.

Shops

Claus Porto

MAP P.60, POCKET MAP C11
Rua da Misericórdia 135.

Portugal's premium soap brand, Claus Porto has been making top-quality toiletries in Porto since 1887. You can sample their full range of beautifully packaged soaps and smellies in this Lisbon branch, housed in an old pharmacy with the original wooden medicine cabinets and tiled floors.

Cork & Co.

MAP P.60, POCKET MAP B12
Rua das Salgadeiras 10
Ⓦ corkandcompany.pt.

Portugal supplies around fifty percent of the world's cork, and this stylish shop displays the versatility of the product with a range of tasteful cork goods, featuring everything from bags and bracelets to umbrellas.

Embaixada

MAP P.60, POCKET MAP A10
Praça do Príncipe Real 26 Ⓦ www.embaixadalx.pt.

Housed in a former pseudo-Moorish palace overlooking Praça do Príncipe Real, this is a beautiful upmarket shopping emporium which showcases some of Portugal's leading designers. Inside you'll find sleek airy spaces selling designer clothes, shoes and contemporary furniture. As you wander around, take in the temporary exhibits dotted about and when you need a refresh, call into the café-bar-restaurant which is located in a wonderfully ornate room or head outside to grab a table on the shaded terrace.

Solar

MAP P.60, POCKET MAP B10
Rua Dom Pedro V 70 Ⓦ solar.com.pt.

A huge treasure trove of antique tiles, plates and ceramics dating back to the sixteenth century – great for a browse.

Restaurants

Antigo Restaurante 1° de Maio

MAP P.60, POCKET MAP B12
Rua da Atalaia 8 ☎ 213 426 840.

This restaurant serves simple home-cooking, such *as* slabs of grilled fish and meat with boiled veg and chips. You can watch the cook through a hatch at the back, adding to the theatrics of a bustling, traditional *adega* (wine cellar) with a low, arched ceiling. Get there early to be sure of a table. €€

Bota Alta

MAP P.60, POCKET MAP B11
Trav da Queimada 37 ☎ 213 427 959.

Tavern decorated with old boots (*botas*) and an eclectic picture collection. It attracts queues of those in the know for its vast portions of sensibly priced, traditional Portuguese food – including *bacalhau com natas* (cod cooked in cream) and fine cakes. The tables are crammed in and it's always packed; try to arrive before 8pm or book in advance. €€

Cervejaria da Trindade

MAP P.60, POCKET MAP C11
Rua Nova da Trindade 20
Ⓦ cervejariatrindade.pt.

Reopened in 2022 after extensive renovation works, the city's oldest beer-hall dates from 1836. Overseen by top chef Alexandre Silva, the restaurant is housed in the original vaulted hall, teh walls of which are decorated with traditional *azulejos* depicting the elements and seasons. Shellfish and steak are the specialities here, though the *petiscaria* also serves lighter dishes such as *pregos*, cheese and charcuterie platters. €€

Comida de Santo

MAP P.60, POCKET MAP H6
Calçada Engenheiro Miguel Pais 39
Ⓦ comidodesanto.pt.

Late-opening Brazilian restaurant serving cocktails and classic dishes such as *feijoada a Brasileira* (Brazilian bean stew) and a fantastic *ensopadinho de peixe* (fish in coconut), with good vegetarian options too. €€

Esplanada

MAP P.60, POCKET MAP A10
Praça do Príncipe Real ☎ 962 311 669.

A good range of burgers, salads and tapas makes this an ideal and inexpensive lunch spot. The outdoor tables set under the trees get snapped up quickly, though the glass pavilion comes into its own when the weather turns. Service can be on the tardy side. €

La Paparrucha

MAP P.60, POCKET MAP B10
Rua Dom Pedro V 18–20
Ⓦ lapaparrucha.com.

The best feature of this Argentinian restaurant is the fantastic back room and terrace offering superb views over the Baixa. The food is recommended too, with steaks, fish and pasta options, and good-value lunchtime buffets. €€

Mini Bar

MAP P.60, POCKET MAP C11
Bairro do Avillez, Rua Nova da Trinade 18
Ⓦ minibar.pt.

There's certainly a theatrical element to the cuisine in this buzzy restaurant, set in an amazing vaulted former chapel and the centrepiece of chef José Avillez's Bairro do Avillez. Various themed tasting menus feature innovative and quirky tapas-style dishes, including Algarve prawns, tuna and mackerel ceviche and beef croquettes. Some of top chef José Avillez's creations are decidedly Blumenthal-esque, including amazing 'edible' cocktails and 'exploding' olives. Highly recommended, there's also occasional live music. €€€€

Páteo

MAP P.60, POCKET MAP C11
Bairro do Avillez, Rua Nova da Trinade 18
Ⓦ bairrodoavillez.pt.

Top chef José Avillez has four lively restaurants in this artfully

Inside Pharmacia Felicidade

BAIRRO ALTO AND SÃO BENTO

Pharmacia Felicidade's elegant exterior

converted former monastery: Páteo is at the heart of the "patio", a beautiful balconied space beneath soaring roof lights. It specialises in fish and seafood, with sublime dishes such as garlic prawns, fish rice and tuna *escabeche*, as well as a few meat and vegetarian dishes. €€€

Pharmacia Felicidade

MAP P.60, POCKET MAP A12
Rua Marechal Saldanha 1 ☎ 213 462 146.
Part of the Pharmaceutical Society and Museum, this traditional building on lawns facing the Tejo is a terrific spot for the quirky café-restaurant decked out with retro pharmacy fittings. The speciality here is tapas and mains such as black pork cheeks. Also good for cocktails. €€

Príncipe Calhariz

MAP P.60, POCKET MAP B12
Calçado do Combro 28–30 ☎ 213 420 971.
Here's a place that's reliable, good value, has plenty of tables, generous portions – and a local buzz. Recommended are the *porco*

Portuguesa (fried pork cubes with fried potatoes) and the salmon steaks. Leave room for the rich chocolate mousse. €€

Taberna

MAP P.60, POCKET MAP C11
Bairro do Avillez, Rua Nova da Trinade 18
ⓦ bairrodoavillez.pt.
The more earthy and affordable of José Avillez's *Bairro* restaurants, set out like an old tavern with cured hams hanging above the bar. But there is nothing downmarket about the cuisine from one of Lisbon's top chefs: choose from a sumptuous array of Portuguese cheeses, hams, sausages and cod dishes. The tuna prego – seared tuna cooked in a bun – is superb. €€

Tasca do Manel

MAP P.60, POCKET MAP B12
Rua da Barroca 24 ☎ 213 463 813.
One of the dying breed of inexpensive *tascas*, still attracting a largely local crowd for wholesome dishes such as wild boar, grilled salmon or bean stew with outdoor seats in summer. €€

Tascardoso

MAP P.60, POCKET MAP A10
Rua Dom Pedro V 137 ☎ 213 427 578.
A long standing favourite, the tiny eating area opposite Praça do Princípe Real serves excellent and inexpensive tapas-style meats and cheeses and good-value hot dishes. €

Cafés

Brotería Café

MAP P.60, POCKET MAP B11
Rua de São Pedro de Alcântara 3. ☎ 213 961 660.
Inside a historic Jesuit college – now a library and cultural centre – this has a small café tucked at the back, with tables in a lovely patio below a lemon tree. There are good value dishes of the day such as prawn kebabs or steaks, and the usual hot and cold drinks. €

Loop

MAP P.52, POCKET MAP H6
Largo Agostginho da Silva 1
Ⓦ looprestaurante.com.
Café, shop and deli specializing in local and seasonal produce, with tables outside facing a small and quiet square. There's usually two dishes of the day – one meat and one vegetarian – plus a range of sharing plates such as vegan moussaka, quiche and pork with plum sauce, as well as a range of drinks, teas and coffees. €€

Lost In

MAP P.60, POCKET MAP B10
Rua Dom Pedro V 56 Ⓦ lostinrestaurante.com.
This little Indian-inspired shop and café-restaurant has a great terrace with exhilarating views over town and occasional live jazz. The menu features Oriental chicken and veggie burgers, or just pop in for a drink. €€

Noobai

MAP P.60, POCKET MAP A12
Miradouro do Adamastor, Rua de Catarina Ⓦ noobaicafe.com.
Modern, jazzy café-restaurant with a superb terrace just below Miradouro de Santa Catarina. Fabulous views complement the inexpensive fresh juices, cocktails, tapas, quiches and the like. €€

Tease

MAP P.60, POCKET MAP H6
Rua Nova da Piedade 15 Ⓦ tease.pt.
Specializing in amazing cupcakes and chocolate goodies, this hip, tiled café with jazzy sounds also teases your tastebuds with juices, smoothies and inexpensive light lunches such as quiches and salads. €

Bars and clubs

A Tasca Tequila Bar

MAP P.60, POCKET MAP C11
Trav da Queimada 13–15 ☎ 915 617 805.
Colourful Mexican bar with Latin sounds, which caters to a good-time crowd downing tequilas, margaritas and Brazilian *caipirinhas*.

Cinco Lounge

MAP P.60, POCKET MAP A11

Drinks at Cinco

Rua Ruben A. Leitão 17a ⓦ cincolounge.com.
A New York-style cocktail lounge
run by Brits in the heart of Lisbon
– there are over a hundred cocktails
to choose from; go for one of the
wacky fruit concoctions (anyone
for tequila, beetroot and lime?)
while sinking into one of the
enormous comfy sofas.

Clube da Esquina

MAP P.60, POCKET MAP B12
Rua da Barroca 30 ⓣ 929 092 742.
Buzzing little corner bar with
ancient radios on the walls and DJs
spinning discs. Attracts a young
crowd enjoying vast measures of
spirits.

Gin Lovers

MAP P.60, POCKET MAP A10
Praça do Príncipe Real 26 ⓦ ginlovers.pt.
This amazing bar-restaurant
nestles inside the internal patio of
the pseudo-Moorish Embaixada
shopping emporium, an opulent
setting for reasonably priced bar
food such as chicken stuffed with
spinach and *bacalhau à bras*. As
the name implies, the speciality
here is gin, with over 60 varieties,

though there are plenty of other
drinks too.

Janela da Atalaia

MAP P.60, POCKET MAP B11
Rua da Atalaia 160 ⓣ 213 465 988.
A fine old bar with two rooms,
inexpensive cocktails – try the rum
with figs and ginger – and laid-back
sounds, usually world music. Most
Wednesdays there's a band, often
salsa/Brazilian.

Mahjong

MAP P.60, POCKET MAP B12
Rua da Atalaia 3 ⓣ 213 421 039.
At the bottom of the Bairro Alto
and traditionally a place to start an
evening before moving on up. It's
a great space, with plain white tiles
and a rough wooden bar juxtaposed
with modern Chinese motifs – the
clientele are similarly eclectic.

Maria Caxuxa

MAP P.60, POCKET MAP B12
Rua da Barroca 12 ⓣ 965 039 094.
This arty lounge-bar has plenty
of space for big sofas and eclectic
decor – including record players
and aged machinery – though these

Bairro Alto

Taking a break in Café Esplanada

get lost in the crowds when the DJ pumps up the volume as the evening progresses.

Park

MAP P.60, POCKET MAP A12
Calçada do Combro 58 ☎ 215 914 011.
Reached via a poky entrance inside a car park, this chic rooftop bar comes as quite a surprise. There are potted plants and trees, great cocktails and bar snacks, and a stunning view across the river. At weekends there are often guest DJs and cultural events.

Pavilhão Chinês

MAP P.60, POCKET MAP B10
Rua Dom Pedro V 89–91 ☎ 213 424 729.
Once a nineteenth-century tea and coffee merchants' shop, this is now a quirky bar set in a series of comfy rooms, including a pool room. Most are lined with mirrored cabinets containing a bizarre range of 4000 artefacts from around the world, including a cabinet of model trams. There's waiter service and the usual drinks are supplemented by a long list of cocktails.

Portas Largas

MAP P.60, POCKET MAP B11
Rua da Atalaia 103–105 ☎ 218 466 379.

The bar's *portas largas* (big doors) are usually thrown wide open, inviting the neighbourhood into this friendly black-and-white-tiled *adega* (wine cellar). There are cheapish drinks, music from fado to pop (sometimes live), and a young, mixed gay and straight clientele, which spills onto the streets.

Music venues

Alface Hall

MAP P.60, POCKET MAP C11
Rua do Norte 96 ☎ 213 433 293.
This quirky café-bar is in a former printworks. Now part of a hostel and filled with retro chairs and artefacts, its high ceilings and comfy sofas make it an ideal place to hang out – they also host live music now and again.

Tasca do Chico

MAP P.60, POCKET MAP B12
Rua do Diário de Notícias 39 ☎ 961 339 696.
Atmospheric little bar filled with football scarves (a fine spot for a drink), which morphs into a very popular fado bar most nights, when crowds pack in to hear moving fado from 8pm.

Estrela, Lapa and Santos

West of the Bairro Alto sits the leafy district of Estrela, best known for its gardens and enormous basilica. To the south lies opulent Lapa, Lisbon's diplomatic quarter, sheltering some of its top hotels. Sumptuous mansions and grand embassy buildings peer out majestically towards the Tejo. The superb Museu Nacional de Arte Antiga below here is Portugal's national gallery, while down on the riverfront, Santos is promoted as "the district of design" with some of the city's coolest shops.

Basílica and Jardim da Estrela

MAP P.73, POCKET MAP G6
Largo da Estrela, Tram #28 or #25, church free, charge for roof visits.

The impressive **Basílica da Estrela** is a vast monument to late eighteenth-century Neoclassicism. Constructed by order of Queen Maria I (whose tomb lies within), and completed in 1790, its landmark white dome can be seen from much of the city. You can visit the flat roof (via 140 steep stone steps) for fine views over the western suburbs, and also walk round the inside of the dome to peer down at the church interior 25 metres below. Opposite is the **Jardim da Estrela** (free), one of the city's most enjoyable gardens with a pond-side café and a well-equipped children's playground.

Cemitério dos Ingleses

MAP P.73, POCKET MAP G6
Rua São Jorge 6, Tram #28 or #25 ☎ 213 906 248, free.

Jardim da Estrela

The English cemetery

"**The English Cemetery**" is actually a cemetery for all Protestants, founded in 1717. Here, among the cypresses and tombs of various expatriates, lie the remains of author Henry Fielding. He came to Lisbon hoping the climate would improve his failing health, but his inability to recuperate may have influenced his verdict on Lisbon as "the nastiest city in the world".

Lapa

MAP P.73, POCKET MAP F7

From Estrela, tram #25 skirts past the well-heeled district of **Lapa** on its way down to the waterfront. Lapa is the most desired address in the city and though it contains no sights as such, it is worth wandering around to admire the stunning mansions. A good route is to follow the tram tracks from Estrela and turn right into Rua do Sacramento à Lapa, past fantastic embassy buildings. Turn left into Rua do Pau da Bandeira past the *Olissippo Lapa Palace* hotel (if you have the funds, have a drink at the bar). From here, go left into Rua do Prior and right into Rua do Conde and it's a ten-minute walk downhill to the Museu Nacional de Arte Antiga (see below).

Museu Nacional de Arte Antiga

MAP P.73, POCKET MAP G8

Rua das Janelas Verdes 95, bus #760 from Praça da Figueira, #727 from Belém or a short walk from tram #25 Ⓦ museudearteantiga.pt, charge.

The **Museu Nacional de Arte Antiga** features the largest collection of Portuguese fifteenth- and sixteenth-century paintings in the country, European art from the fourteenth century to the present day, and a rich display of applied art. All of this is well exhibited in a tastefully converted seventeenth-century palace once owned by the Marquês de Pombal. The museum uses ten "reference points" to guide you round the collection. The principal highlight is **Nuno Gonçalves's altarpiece** dedicated to St Vincent (1467–70), a brilliantly marshalled composition depicting Lisbon's patron saint receiving homage from all ranks of its citizens, their faces appearing remarkably modern. The other main highlight is Hieronymus

Santos district

century St Albert monastery, most of which was razed during the 1755 earthquake, although its beautiful chapel can still be seen today, downstairs by the main entrance. Don't miss the garden café, either (see page 75).

Museu da Marioneta

MAP P.73, POCKET MAP G7
Rua da Esperança 146, Tram #25 then a short walk ⓦ museudamarioneta.pt, charge.

Contemporary and historical **puppets** from around the world are displayed and demonstrated in this former eighteenth-century convent, now a well-laid-out **museum**. Highlights include shadow puppets from Turkey and Indonesia, string marionettes, Punch and Judy-style puppets and almost life-sized, faintly disturbing modern figures by Portuguese puppeteer Helena Vaz, which are anything but cute. There are also video displays and projections, masks from Africa and Asia, while the final room exhibits Wallace and Gromit-style plasticine figures with demonstrations on how they are manipulated for films.

Santos

MAP P.73, POCKET MAP G7
Santos was traditionally a run-down riverside area of factories and warehouses where people only ventured after dark because of its nightclubs. Over the years, artists and designers moved into the inexpensive and expansive warehouse spaces, and now Santos has a reputation as the city's designer heartland. Its riverside streets are not particularly alluring, but you can see many of the country's top designers showcasing their products in various shops and galleries. Fashionable bars and restaurants have followed in their wake, though the area around the Museu da Marioneta retains an earthy, villagey feel to its cobbled backstreets.

Bosch's stunningly gruesome *Temptation of St Anthony* in room 57 (don't miss the image on the back of the painting, showing the arrest of Christ). Elsewhere, seek out the altar panel depicting the *Resurrection* by Raphael; Francisco de Zurbarán's *The Twelve Apostles;* a small statue of a nymph by Auguste Rodin; and works by Dürer, Holbein, Cranach (particularly *Salome*), Fragonard and Josefa de Óbidos, considered one of Portugal's greatest female painters.

The **Oriental art** collection shows how the Portuguese were influenced by overseas designs encountered during the sixteenth century. There is inlaid furniture from Goa, Turkish and Syrian *azulejos*, Qing Dynasty porcelain and a fantastic series of late sixteenth-century Japanese *namban* screens (room 14), depicting the Portuguese landing at Nagasaki. The Japanese regarded the Portuguese traders as southern barbarians (*namban*) with large noses – hence their Pinocchio-like features. The museum extends over the remains of the sixteenth-

ESTRELA, LAPA AND SANTOS

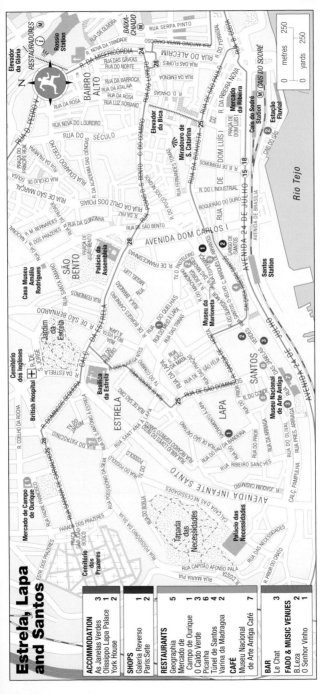

Estrela, Lapa and Santos

ACCOMMODATION	
As Janelas Verdes	3
Olisippo Lapa Palace	1
York House	2

SHOPS	
Galeria Reverso	1
Paris:Sete	2

RESTAURANTS	
Geographia	5
Mercado de Campo de Ourique	1
O Caldo Verde	3
Picanha	6
Túnel de Santos	4
Varina da Madragoa	2

CAFÉ	
Museu Nacional de Arte Antiga Café	7

BAR	
Le Chat	3

FADO & MUSIC VENUES	
B.Leza	2
O Senhor Vinho	1

Shops

Galeria Reverso

MAP P.73, POCKET MAP H7

Rua da Esperança 59–61 ☎ 919 809 131.
Jewellery workshop and gallery managed by well-known Portuguese designer Paula Crespo, whose big, heavy jewellery is eye-catching. International designers also feature, many using unusual materials such as rubber and wood, though to buy anything you'll need a deep purse.

Paris:Sete

MAP P.73, POCKET MAP H7

Largo Vitorino Damásio 2C ⓦ paris-sete. com.
Bright, white space selling designer furniture and curios, with heavyweight names such as Charles and Ray Eames and Philippe Starck behind some of them.

Restaurants

Geographia

MAP P.73, POCKET MAP F8

Rua do Conde 1 ⓦ restaurantegeographia. pt.
As you would expect from the name, this is a travel-themed restaurant specializing in tasty food from Portugal's former colonies, with a cosy, pub-like interior. The wide range of dishes include Rolom soup with tuna from Cape Verde, braised fish with okra and spinach from Angola, black pork with saffron rice from East Timor and caramelized banana cake from São Tomé. There are also dishes from Brazil and Mozambique, not to mention some interesting cocktails: try the Portuguese gin with *ginginha*. €€

Mercado de Campo de Ourique

MAP P.73, POCKET MAP F6

Rua Coelho da Rocha 104 ☎ 211 323 701.
This wonderful 1930s building has been given a revamp and now not only sells fish, fruit and veg, but also shelters around twenty *tasquinhas* (small food stalls) serving pastries, sushi, *petiscos*, burgers and seafood. There are also bars (gin cocktails, flavoured teas and the like) and occasional live entertainment in the evenings. €

O Caldo Verde

MAP P.73, POCKET MAP G7

Rua da Esperança 91 ☎ 213 903 581.
This charming little local is rated by Portuguese newspaper *Expresso* as serving some of the best grilled sardines in the city, though its other dishes – such as hake fillets and chunky steaks – are equally good. Don't miss its speciality *caldo verde* (cabbage soup). €€

Picanha

MAP P.73, POCKET MAP G8

Rua das Janelas Verdes 96 ☎ 213 975 401.
This ornately tiled restaurant specializes in *picanha* (strips of beef in garlic sauce) accompanied by black-eyed beans, salad and potatoes. Great if this appeals to you, since for a fixed-price deal you can eat all you want; otherwise forget it, as that's all that is on offer. €€

Túnel de Santos

MAP P.73, POCKET MAP G7

Largo de Santos 1 ☎ 912 151 850.
Lively, modern café-restaurant with brick vaulted ceilings and outdoor seating facing the square, attracting a young crowd for inexpensive grills, snacks and salads. €€

Varina da Madragoa

MAP P.73, POCKET MAP G7

Rua das Madres 34 ☎ 213 965 533.
A delightfully simple local that's hosted the likes of fomer US President Jimmy Carter and Portuguese PM José Sócrates, and it's easy to see why they liked it: a lovely, traditional restaurant

Le Chat

with grape-motif *azulejos* on the walls and a menu featuring dishes such as *bacalhau*, trout and steaks. Desserts include a splendid almond ice cream with hot chocolate sauce. €€

Café

Museu Nacional de Arte Antiga Café

MAP P.73, POCKET MAP G8
Rua das Janelas Verdes 95 ⊕ 213 912 860.
There's no need to visit the museum to use its fantastic café – go in through the museum exit opposite Largo Dr J de Figueiredo and head to the basement. Lunches and drinks can be enjoyed in a superb garden studded with statues and overlooking Lisbon's docks. €

Bar

Le Chat

MAP P.73, POCKET MAP F8
Jardim 9 de Abril ⊕ 213 963 668.
A modern, glass-sided bar-restaurant adjacent to the Museu

Nacional de Arte Antiga, *Le Chat* has a terrific terrace which gazes over the docks and Ponte 25 de Abril. Great at any time of the day, it's a particularly fine spot for a cocktail or sundowner.

Fado and music venues

B.Leza

MAP P.73, POCKET MAP A14
Cais da Ribeira Nova Armazém B ⊚ bleza.pt.
A great African club, with live music, poetry nights, *kizomba* evenings and occasional dance lessons on offer, though you'd be hard pushed to outshine the regulars.

O Senhor Vinho

MAP P.73, POCKET MAP G7
Rua do Meio à Lapa 18 ⊚ srvinho.com.
In the fashionable Madragoa district, this famous fado club features some of the best singers in Portugal (from 9pm), hence the high prices (around €50 a head). Reservations are advised.

Alcântara and the docks

Loomed over by the enormous Ponte 25 de Abril suspension bridge, Alcântara has a decidedly industrial hue, with a tangle of flyovers and cranes from the docks dominating the skyline. The area is well known for its nightlife, thanks mainly to its dockside warehouse conversions that shelter cafés and restaurants. It also hosts a couple of fine museums, both tipping their hats to Portugal's historic links with the Far East and there's an attractive riverside promenade. To get to the docks, take a train from Cais do Sodré to Alcântara-Mar or tram #15.

Museu do Oriente

MAP P.78, POCKET MAP E8
Avda de Brasília Ⓦ foriente.pt. charge, free Fri 6–8pm.

Owned by the powerful Orient Foundation, this spacious **museum** traces the cultural links that Portugal has built up with its former colonies in Macao, India, East Timor and other Asian countries. Housed in an enormous 1930s Estado Novo building, highlights of the extensive collection include valuable nineteenth-century Chinese porcelain, an amazing array of seventeenth-century Chinese snuff boxes and, from the same century, Japanese armour and entire carved pillars from Goa. The top floor is given over to displays on the Gods of Asia, featuring a bright collection of religious costumes and shrines used in Bali and Vietnam together with Taoist altars, statues of Buddha, some fine Japanese Shinto masks and Indonesian

Treasures in the Museu do Oriente

Doca de Santo Amaro

shadow puppets. Vivid images of Hindu gods Shiva, Ganesh the elephant god and Kali the demon are counterbalanced by some lovely Thai amulets. There is also a decent top-floor restaurant.

Doca de Santo Amaro

MAP P.78, POCKET MAP D9

Just west of the Doca de Alcântara lies the more intimate **Doca de Santo Amaro**, nestling right under the humming traffic and rattling trains crossing Ponte 25 de Abril. This small, almost completely enclosed marina is filled with bobbing sailing boats and lined with tastefully converted warehouses. Its international cafés and restaurants are pricier than usual for Lisbon, but the constant comings and goings of the Tejo provide plenty of free entertainment. Leaving Doca de Santo Amaro at its western side, you can pick up a pleasant riverside path that leads all the way to Belém (see page 82), twenty minutes' walk west, or follow the slightly more urban cycle route around a 30-minute walk east to Praça do Comércio.

Ponte 25 de Abril and the Pilar 7 Experience

MAP P.78. POCKET MAP D9
Avenida da India ☎ 211 117 880, charge.

Resembling the Golden Gate Bridge in San Francisco, the hugely impressive **Ponte 25 de Abril** was opened in 1966 as a vital link between Lisbon and the southern banks of the Tejo. Around 2.3km in length, the bridge rises to 70m above the river, though its main pillars are nearly 200m tall. It was originally named Ponte de Salazar after the dictatorial prime minister who ruled Portugal with an iron fist from 1932 to 1968, but took its present name to mark the date of the revolution that overthrew Salazar's regime in 1974. The dizzying **Pilar 7 Experience** offers the opportunity to ascend 70m up one of the bridge's pillars to a glass-encased platform for a close-up look at the thundering traffic and stunning views across the western riverfront. Inside, an exhibition space traces the history of the bridge using models and multimedia, including a somewhat grainy projection room detailing how three thousand workers built the bridge using 55,000km of steel wire. For an extra €1.50, you can experience a virtual-reality recreation of how maintenance workers carry out repairs on the central pillars, a hairy 200m above the river. Note that visitor numbers are restricted to 100 at any one time (and only 40 on the viewpoint).

Museu do Centro Científico e Cultural de Macau

MAP P.78, POCKET MAP C9
Rua da Junqueira 30 ⓦ cccm.gov.pt, charge.

This attractively laid-out **museum** is dedicated to Portugal's historical **trading links** with the Orient and, specifically, its former colony of Macau, which was handed back to Chinese rule in 1999. There are model boats and audio displays detailing early sea voyages, as well as various historic journals and artefacts, including a seventeenth-century portable wooden altar, used

by travelling clergymen. Upstairs, exhibitions of Chinese art from the sixteenth to the nineteenth centuries show off ornate collections of porcelain, silverware and applied art, most notably an impressive array of opium pipes and ivory boxes.

Museu da Carris

MAP P.78, POCKET MAP D8
Rua 1° de Maio 101 ⓦ museu.carris.pt, charge.

This engagingly quirky and ramshackle **museum** traces the history of Lisbon's **public transport**, from the earliest trams and street lifts to the development of the metro. There are three zones, the first with evocative black-and-white photos, uniforms and models. You then hop on a real tram dating from 1901 which takes you to a warehouse filled with historic trams, and then on to another warehouse with ancient buses and models of metro trains. It's especially great fun

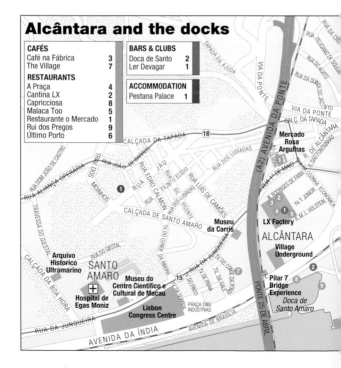

Alcântara and the docks

CAFÉS			BARS & CLUBS	
Café na Fábrica	3		Doca de Santo	2
The Village	7		Ler Devagar	1
RESTAURANTS				
A Praça	4		**ACCOMMODATION**	
Cantina LX	2		Pestana Palace	1
Capricciosa	8			
Malaca Too	5			
Restaurante o Mercado	1			
Rui dos Pregos	9			
Último Porto	6			

for kids, who can clamber on board and pretend to drive the vehicles. The bottom of the site also has the eye-catching **Village Underground**, a bizarre medley of old shipping containers and double-decker buses now given over to workspaces for writers and artists.

LX Factory

MAP P.78, POCKET MAP D8
Rua Rodrigues Faria 103 ⓦ lxfactory.com.
Below Ponte 25 de Abril, this former nineteenth-century industrial estate is now the place to test Lisbon's creative pulse. The factories and warehouses have turned into a mini-district of workshops and studios for the city's go-getters, along with a series of superb boutiques, shops, cafés and bars set in fashionably run-down urban spaces. Sunday afternoon is a good time to visit, with a lively flea market and many places open for brunch: **LX Factory**'s Open

LX Factory

Days take place throughout the year, featuring shows, live music and film screenings (check website for details).

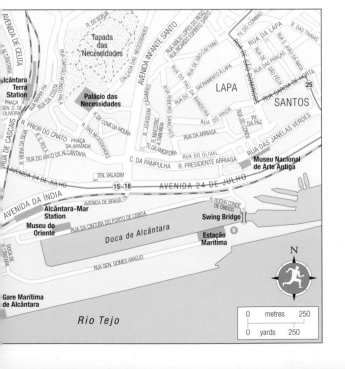

Cafés

Café na Fábrica

MAP P.78, POCKET MAP D8
LX Factory, Rua Rodrigues Faria 103 ☎ 967 382 848.

Set in a small but inviting wooden warehouse, this arty space is a very popular place to go for lunch, serving up delicious wraps, quiches, baguettes and a selection of salads. There are also a few outdoor tables to make the most of fine weather. €

The Village

MAP P.78, POCKET MAP D9
Village Underground, Avenida da Índia 52 ☎ 215 832 469.

Grab a burger, wrap or *prego* (steak in a bun) or just a drink in Village Underground at the eclectic Museu de Carris (see page 79), where the kitchens and seating are inside an old double-decker bus. There are also plenty of outdoor tables where you can sit alongside Lisbon's cool, creative crowd, and there's regular live music and entertainment at the venue, too. €

Restaurants

A Praça

MAP P.78, POCKET MAP D8
LX Factory, Edifício H, Espaço 001 ☎ 210 991 792.

One of the larger restaurants in LX Factory, a hip spot with an open kitchen serving a range of dishes, including pasta, steaks and seafood. It also does good cocktails. €€

Cantina LX

MAP P.78, POCKET MAP D8
LX Factory, Rua Rodrigues Faria 103 ☎ 213 628 239.

Upcycled furniture and bench-like tables in a spacious former warehouse make this a hip spot. Great breakfasts, snacks and daily specials which usually focus on healthy salads.

Capricciosa

MAP P.78, POCKET MAP D9
Doca de Santo Amaro Armazém 8 ⓦ capricciosa.com.pt.

Set inside a bright former warehouse, *Capricciosa* serves

A bar in LX Factory

good value 'artestan' pizzas as well as pasta and salads. Next to a pedestrianized walkway around the marina, this is always popular with families; try and bag one of the alluring tables facing the bobbing boats of the marina. €€

Malaca Too

MAP P.78, POCKET MAP D8
LX Factory, Rua Rodrigues Faria 103, Edifício G-03 ☎ 213 477 082.
This fantastic space has tables wedged between giant old printing presses – a surprising backdrop for fresh, Oriental cuisine ranging from wanton soup and green curries to fresh fish. €€

Restaurante o Mercado

MAP P.78, POCKET MAP D8
Mercado Rosa Agulhas, Rua Leão de Oliveira, Loja 19 ⓦ restauranteomercado. pt.
On three floors by the market building – and Lisbon's markets are always worth a call – this is a great place to have a hearty meal. The ingredients don't have far to travel: the fish and vegetables are day-fresh, and there's a long list of grilled meats and seafood, including a fine seafood pasta. €€

Rui dos Pregos

MAP P.78, POCKET MAP D9
Passeio Doca de Santo Amaro ⓦ ruidospregos.pt.
One of the less pricey options set to one side of the docks, with appealing outdoor tables. The speciality here is *pregos* (beef sandwiches), with various varieties and combinations. €

Último Porto

MAP P.78, POCKET MAP F8
Estação Marítima da Rocha Conde de Óbidos ☎ 213 979 498.
Perched at the edge of Lisbon's main container shipping docks, this earthy lunchtime restaurant ('the last port') is popular with the local dock workers who come here at lunchtimes for inexpensive grilled

Ler Devagar

fish; the sardines are hard to beat and portions are generous. €€

Bars and clubs

Doca de Santo

MAP P.78, POCKET MAP D8
Armazém CP, Doca de Santo Amaro ☎ 213 963 535.
Though it's located slightly away from the river, this palm-fringed venue is worth seeking out; there's an enticing cocktail bar on the esplanade, while the restaurant inside serves well-priced modern Portuguese food (grilled fish and meats with pasta or couscous).

Ler Devagar

MAP P.78, POCKET MAP D8
LX Factory, Rua Rodrigues Faria 103, Edifício G-03 ⓦ lerdevagar.com.
Primarily a wonderful arts bookshop, with shelves reaching an old printing press, this also has a corner café-bar, a great place to sample Portuguese wines by the glass. It also hosts exhibits and occasional live music.

Belém and Ajuda

With its maritime history and attractive riverside location, Belém (pronounced ber-layng) is understandably one of Lisbon's most popular suburbs. It was from Belém that Vasco da Gama famously set sail for India in 1497. The monastery subsequently built here – the Mosteiro dos Jerónimos – stands as a testament to his triumphant discovery of a sea route to the Orient, which initiated the beginning of a Portuguese golden age. Along with the monastery and the landmark Torre de Belém, the suburb boasts a group of small museums, including the fantastic Berardo Collection of modern art. Just to the northeast of Belém is Ajuda, famed for its palace and ancient botanical gardens. Higher still lies the extensive parkland of Monsanto, Lisbon's largest green space.

Praça do Império
MAP P.84, POCKET MAP C4

The formal walkways and gardens that make up **Praça do Império** are laid out over Belém's former beach. It's a popular spot, especially on Saturday mornings, when there are often weddings taking place at the monastery, whose photocalls invariably spill out into the square. The seventeenth-century buildings along Rua Vieira Portuense are now mostly restaurants with outdoor seating; as a rule, the further east you head, the better value they become.

The fabulous Praça do Império

Belém transport

You can reach Belém on tram #15 (signed Algés), which runs from Praça da Figueira via Praça do Comércio (20min). Ask at the ticket offices of the main sites about combined tickets that can save money on entry to the main attractions, which all attract long queues in the summer. You can also take a hop-on, hop-off bus tour (☎ 211 117 880; €17 valid for 24 hours) around the suburb's main sights, including the Ponte 25 Abril. Alternatively, hire bikes (🌐 biclas.com) from the kiosk 5min east of the MAAT (see page 87).

Jardim do Ultramar and Presidência da República

MAP P.84, POCKET MAP C4
Garden entrance on Calçada do Galvão
☎ 213 609 660, charge.

The leafy **Jardim do Ultramar** is an oasis of hothouses, ponds and towering palms, a lovely place for a shady walk. In the southeastern corner lies the President's official residence, the pink **Presidência da República**, which opens its state rooms for guided visits on Saturdays (entrance on Praça Afonso de Albuquerque, 🌐 museu. presidencia.pt, free).

Museu de Arte Popular

MAP P.84, POCKET MAP B5
Avda de Brasília 🌐 museuartepopular. wordpress.com, charge.

In a space which feels slightly too large for its exhibits, this charming **museum** chronicles Portugal's **folk art**, from beautiful wood and cork toys to ceramics, rugs and fascinating traditional costumes, including amazing cloaks from the Trás-os-Montes region.

Mosteiro dos Jerónimos

MAP P.84, POCKET MAP C4
Praça do Império 🌐 mosteirojeronimos. gov.pt, charge.

If there's one building that symbolizes the Golden Age of the Portuguese discoveries, it's the **Mosteiros dos Jerónimos**, which is also considered to be the first ever Manueline building. Now a UNESCO World Heritage Site,

the monastery and its adjacent church were built to fulfill a promise that Portugal's king, Dom Manuel, made, should Vasco da Gama return safely from his inaugural voyage to India in 1498. Construction began in 1502 under the architect Diogo de Boitaca.

Appropriately, Vasco da Gama's tomb now lies just inside the fantastically embellished entrance to the church. Crowned by an elaborate medley of statues, including Henry the Navigator, the 32-metre-high entrance was designed by the Spaniard João de Castilho, who took over the building of the church in 1517. The interior is even more dazzling, displaying the maritime influences typical of Manueline architecture – the escutcheons on its ceiling come from the actual ships that sailed the voyages of exploration. The church also contains the tomb of Luís de Camões (1527–1570), Portugal's greatest poet and recorder of the discoveries, alongside the tombs of former presidents and dignitaries.

Equally impressive is the adjacent monastery, gathered round sumptuously vaulted cloisters with nautical symbols carved into the honey-coloured limestone. You can still see the twelve niches where navigators stopped for confessionals before their voyages, until the Hieronymite monks were forced out during the dissolution of 1833. In 2007, the monastery was again influential in blessing future trade: the Treaty of Lisbon was signed here to cement the format of the European Union.

Museu de Arqueologia

MAP P.84, POCKET MAP C4
Praça do Império ⓦ museuarqueologia. gov.pt, charge.

Housed in a neo-Manueline extension to the monastery added in 1850, the **archeology museum** has a small section on Egyptian antiquities dating from 6000 BC, but concentrates on Portuguese archeological finds. It's a sparse collection reprieved by coins and jewellery through the ages, and a few fine Roman mosaics. The museum is closed for renovations until 2025.

Museu da Marinha

MAP P.84, POCKET MAP B4
Praça do Império ⓦ bit.ly/MuseuMarinha, charge.

In the west wing of the monastery extension is an absorbing and gargantuan **maritime museum**, packed not only with models of ships, naval uniforms and artefacts from Portugal's Oriental colonies, but also with real vessels – among them fishing boats and sumptuous state barges, plus early seaplanes. Much of the collection comes from that of King Luís I (1861–1889), a keen oceanographer.

Centro Cultural de Belém

MAP P.84, POCKET MAP B4
Praça do Império ⓦ ccb.pt.

The stylish, modern, pink marble **Centro Cultural de Belém** was built to host Lisbon's 1992 presidency of the European Union. It's now one of the city's main cultural centres, containing the Berardo Collection (see page 85) and hosting regular photography and art exhibitions, as well as concerts and shows.

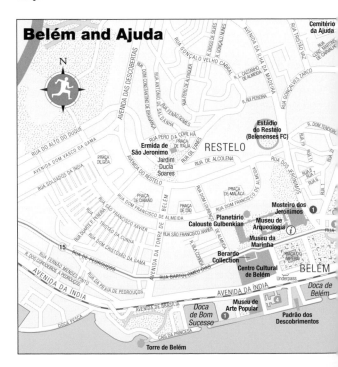

Berardo Collection

MAP P.84, POCKET MAP B4
Entrance via Centro Cultural de Belém,
Praça do Império Ⓦ museuberardo.pt,
charge, free first Sun of each month.

As impressive as Belém's historical
monuments is this unique
collection of modern art amassed
by wealthy Madeiran Joe Berardo,
Portugal's answer to Charles
Saatchi or François Pinault. You
can enjoy some of the world's top
modern artists, though not all of
the vast collection is on display
at the same time. Depending on
when you visit, you may see Eric
Fischl's giant panels of sunbathers;
Andy Warhol's distinctive *Judy
Garland*; and Chris Ofili's
Adoration of Captain Shit,
made with genuine dung, and
the equally controversial *HMS
Cockshitter* by The Chapman
Brothers. Francis Bacon, David
Hockney, Picasso, Míro, Man
Ray, Max Ernst, Dalí, Louise

Art displays in Berardo Collection

Bourgeois and Mark Rothko
also feature, along with various
video artists.

RESTAURANTS	
Marisqueira a Vela	3
Portugália	4
CAFÉS	
MAAT café and kitchen	2
Pastéis de Belém	1
BAR	
Á Margem	1
ACCOMMODATION	
Jéronimos 8	1

Padrão dos Descobrimentos

MAP P.84, POCKET MAP C5
Avda de Brasília, reached via an underpass beneath the Avda da Índia Ⓦ padraodosdescobrimentos.pt, charge.

The **Padrão dos Descobrimentos** (Monument to the Discoveries) is a 54m-high, caravel-shaped slab of concrete erected in 1960 to commemorate the 500th anniversary of the death of Henry the Navigator. A large and detailed statue of Henry appears at the head of a line of statues that feature King Alfonso V, Luís de Camões, Vasco da Gama and other Portuguese heroes. Inside is a small exhibition space which often features displays on Lisbon's history – the entrance fee also includes a ride in the lift providing fine views of the Tejo and the Torre de Belém. Just in front of the monument, tourists pose on the marble pavement decorated with a map of the world charting the routes taken by the great Portuguese explorers.

Torre de Belém

Torre de Belém

MAP P.84, POCKET MAP A5
Avda de Brasília Ⓦ torrebelem.gov.pt, charge.

Reached via a narrow walkway and jutting into the river, the impressive **Torre de Belém** (Tower of Belém) has become an iconic symbol of Lisbon. It is fashioned in the Manueline style that was prominent during the reign of Manuel, its windows and stairways embellished with arches and decorative symbols representing Portugal's explorations into the New World. Built as a fortress to defend the mouth of the River Tejo, it took five years to complete, though when it opened in 1520 it would have been near the centre of the river – the earthquake of 1755 shifted the river's course. Today, visitors are free to explore the tower's various levels, which include a terrace facing the river from where artillery would have been fired. You can then climb a very steep spiral staircase up

MAAT

four levels – each with a slightly different framed view of the river – to a top terrace where you get a blowy panorama of Belém. You can also duck into the dungeons, a low-ceilinged room used to store gunpowder; these were also used notoriously by Dom Miguel to lock up political prisoners in the nineteenth century.

Museu dos Coches

MAP P.84, POCKET MAP D4
Avda Índia 136 and Praça Afonso de Albuquerque ⓦ museudoscoches.gov. pt, charge (combination ticket available including Royal Riding School), free Sun am.
Housed in a vast contemporary building, the **Museu dos Coches** (Coach Museum) contains one of the world's largest collections of carriages and saddlery, including a rare sixteenth-century coach designed for King Felipe I. Heavily gilded, ornate and often beautifully painted, the royal carriages, sedan chairs and children's cabriolets dating from the sixteenth to nineteenth centuries, contrast with the stark modern building, which gives great views over Belém and the river. More coaches from the collection are on display in the former Royal Riding School across the road, though it's only really the

historic building itself that warrants the additional entrance fee.

MAAT (Museum of Art, Architecture and Technology)

MAP P.84, POCKET MAP D4
Avda de Brasília ⓦ www.maat.pt, charge, free first Sun of the month.
British architect Amanda Levete has designed a sumptuous modern building on the riverfront to house the innovative **MAAT**. It's connected to the former Museu da Electricidade next door, a disused red-brick, early-twentieth-century power station, to give eight galleries of exhibition space dedicated to contemporary designers, artists and architects. Regularly changing exhibits feature the likes of Charles and Ray Eames and French artist Dominique Gonzalez-Foerster, while the permanent art collection showcases works by around 250 contemporary Portuguese artists. But as interesting as the exhibits can be, it is the striking building that's really captured people's imagination; a fluid, curving structure covered in 15,000 ceramic tiles that seems to glow at sunset. The galleries (including the giant Oval Room for the show-stopping exhibits) are sunk below street level,

which means you can easily walk up onto the cantilevered roof for wonderful views across the river, and there's also a café-restaurant (see page 89).

Palácio da Ajuda and Royal Treasury Museum

MAP P.84, POCKET MAP D2
Largo da Ajuda. Tram #18 from Praça do Comércio or bus #729 from Belém. Palace: Ⓦ bit.ly/PalacioAjuda, charge; Royal Treasury Museum: Ⓦ tesouroreal.pt, charge (combined ticket available for both places).

This massive **nineteenth-century palace** sits on a hillside above Belém. Construction began in 1802 but was left incomplete when João VI and the royal family fled to Brazil to escape Napoleon's invading army in 1807. The original plans were therefore never fulfilled, though the completed section was used as a royal residence after João returned from exile in 1821. The crashingly tasteless decor was commissioned by the nineteenth-century royal, Dona Maria II (João's granddaughter), and gives an insight into the opulent life the royals lived. The Queen's bedroom comes complete with a polar bear-skin rug, while the throne and ballroom are impressive for their sheer size and extravagance. The highly ornate banqueting hall, full of crystal chandeliers, is also breathtaking. The west wing of the palace now hosts the strikingly modern Royal Treasury Museum, with one of the world's largest vaults built to house around 1,000 pieces of royal pomp, including the Portuguese crown jewels, royal works of art and some of the gold and gemstones plundered from the early days of the colonisation of Brazil.

Jardim Botânico da Ajuda

MAP P.84, POCKET MAP C2
Entrance on Calçada da Ajuda and Calçada do Galvão Ⓦ isa.ulisboa.pt, charge.

A classic example of formal Portuguese gardening, this is one of the city's oldest and most interesting **botanical gardens**. Commissioned by the Marquês de Pombal and laid out in 1768, it was owned by the royal family until the birth of the Republic in 1910, then substantially restored in the 1990s. The garden is divided into eight parts planted with species from around the world, arranged around terraces, statues and fountains, much of it with lovely river views. It also has a nice café.

Páteo Alfacinha

MAP P.84, POCKET MAP D2
Rua do Guarda Jóias 44 Ⓦ pateoalfacinha. com.

Just five minutes' walk from the Palácio da Ajuda, it is worth seeking out this highly picturesque *páteo* – a renovated cluster of traditional nineteenth-century Lisbon houses gathered round a central patio. These were common in the days when families lived in tight-knit communities who looked after and traded with each other. Today the houses only come alive for special events and private parties, often at weekends, though there are two decent restaurants, one which is open in summer and the other in winter.

Parque Florestal de Monsanto

MAP P.84, POCKET MAP E2
Bus #729 from Ajuda or Belém.

The extensive hillside **Parque Florestal de Monsanto** – home to the city's main and well-equipped campsite (Ⓦ lisboacamping.com) – is known as "Lisbon's lungs" though it used to be infamous for the prostitutes who worked here until the Mayor of Lisbon bought a house nearby in 2003. Suddenly the park was given a new lease of life and the hookers have been replaced by horse-and-trap rides to its splendid viewpoints. At weekends in summer it's traffic-free and pop concerts are often laid on, usually free of charge.

The must-try pastéis de Belém

Restaurants

Marisqueira a Vela

MAP P.84, POCKET MAP B9
Avenida de Brasilia Doca de Recreio ☎ 213 642 711.

This bustling restaurant is tucked into the back of the sailing school, with outdoor tables beside the river. It's far enough from the tourist sights to attract a largely local clientele enjoying fresh fish and meat dishes; try the *arroz de lagosta* (lobster rice) for two. €€

Portugália

MAP P.84, POCKET MAP C4
Avda de Brasilia Edif. Espelho d'Água ⓦ portugalia.pt.

Marooned on a little island in an artificial lake facing the Padrão dos Descobrimentos, this glass-fronted restaurant (part of a popular chain), has a serene position. Dishes include *bitoques* (small steaks) and a wonderful *gambas à brás* (prawns with stick potatoes and onions). €€

Cafés

MAAT Café & Kitchen

MAP P.84, POCKET MAP B9
Museum of Art, Architecture and Technology, Avenida de Brasilia ⓦ bit.ly/MAATCafe.

Sleek and stylish, the MAAT's café and restaurant sit below the museum's sweeping roof, superbly framing the pleasant river views. The café, with outdoor seating, serves an array of drinks and snacks (the *pastéis de nata* tartlets are superb), while the adjacent restaurant serves expensive fish and seafood. €€

Pasteis de Belém

MAP P.84, POCKET MAP C4
Rua de Belém 84–92 ⓦ pasteisdebelem.pt.

No visit to Belém is complete without a coffee and hot *pastel de nata* (Portuguese custard tart) liberally sprinkled with *canela* (cinnamon) in this cavernous, tiled pastry shop and café, which has been serving them up since 1837. The place positively heaves, especially at weekends, but there's usually space to sit down in its warren of rooms. €

Bar

Á Margem

MAP P.84, POCKET MAP B5
Doca do Bom Sucesso ⓦ amargem.com.

Chic and minimalist café-bar with stunning views across the river – tables spill out onto the waterfront. Sandwiches plus tapas and salads, and a good list of cocktails and wines. It's near the brick-striped stumpy lighthouse.

Avenida, Parque Eduardo VII and the Gulbenkian

Lisbon's main avenue, Avenida da Liberdade (simply known as "Avenida"), links the centre with its principal park, Parque Eduardo VII, best known for its views and enormous hothouses. The avenue, together with its side streets, was once home to statesmen and public figures. On its western side is the historic Praça das Amoreiras, the finishing point of the massive Águas Livres aqueduct. Here you'll find the Árpád Szenes-Vieira da Silva Foundation, a collection of works by two artists heavily influenced by Lisbon. Northwest of the park, the Fundação Calouste Gulbenkian is undoubtedly Portugal's premier cultural centre, featuring one of Europe's richest art collections. Art-lovers have a further attraction to the east, where you can view the historic paintings and objects in the Casa Museu Dr Anastácio Gonçalves. Just north of here is the bullring at Campo Pequeno, while east lies the city's zoo.

Avenida da Liberdade

MAP P.92, POCKET MAP J5

The 1.3km, palm-lined **Avenida da Liberdade** is still much as poet Fernando Pessoa described it: "the finest artery in Lisbon… full of trees… small gardens, ponds, fountains, cascades and statues". It was laid out in 1882 as the city's main north–south avenue and has several appealing outdoor cafés beneath the shade of trees that help cushion the roar of the passing traffic. Some of the avenue's original nineteenth-century mansions remain, though most have been replaced by modern buildings. The upper end of the avenue (Lisbon's most expensive real estate) houses many of the city's designer shops and ends in a swirl of traffic at the landmark roundabout of Praça Marquês de Pombal, also known as Rotunda.

Parque Mayer

MAP P.92, POCKET MAP J5

Opened in 1922 as an "entertainment precinct" when theatres were all the rage, the fine Art Deco entry pillars of the little **Parque Mayer** lead you to the Teatro Maria Vitória and the recently renovated **Teatro Capitólio** (Portugal's first great Modernist structure), both of which show various plays and shows. It also has a fine restaurant, A Gina (see page 99).

Casa Museu Medeiros e Almeida

MAP P.92, POCKET MAP H5
Rua Rosa Araújo 41 ⓦ casa-museumedeirosealmeida.pt, charge.

This excellent **museum** was the home of the industrialist, philanthropist and art collector **António Medeiros** until his death in 1986. Today it serves as a showcase for his priceless series of artefacts. His collection of 225 Chinese porcelain items (some 2000 years old), sixteenth- to nineteenth-century watches, and English and Portuguese silverware is considered the most valuable in the world. Other highlights include glorious eighteenth-century *azulejos* in the Sala de Lago, a room complete with large water fountains; and a rare seventeenth-century clock, made for Queen Catherine of Bragança and mentioned by Samuel Pepys in his diary.

Praça das Amoreiras

MAP P.92, POCKET MAP G5

One of Lisbon's most tranquil squares, **Praça das Amoreiras** – complete with kids' play area – is dominated on its western side by the Águas Livres aqueduct (see page 94), with a chapel wedged into its arches.

On the south side the **Mãe d'Água** cistern (☏ 218 100 215, charge) marks the end of the line for the aqueduct. Built between 1746 and 1834, the castellated stone building contains a reservoir that once supplied the city. The

structure nowadays hosts occasional temporary art exhibitions. Head to the back where there are stairs leading on to the roof for great views over the city. Back on the square, the little kiosk café is a popular spot for a coffee or beer, and also hosts occasional art exhibits.

Árpád Szenes-Vieira da Silva Foundation

MAP P.92, POCKET MAP G5
Praça das Amoreiras 56–58 ⓦ fasvs.pt, charge.

Árpád Szenes-Vieira da Silva Foundation is a small but highly appealing gallery dedicated to the works of two painters and the artists who have been influenced by them. Arpad Szenes (1897–1985) was a Hungarian-born artist and friend of Henri Matisse and Pierre Bonnard, among others. While in Paris in 1928 he met the Portuguese artist Maria Helena Vieira da Silva (1908–92), whose work was influenced by the surrealism of Joan Miró and Max

AVENIDA, PARQUE EDUARDO VII AND THE GULBENKIAN

Mãe d'Água cistern, Praça das Amoreiras

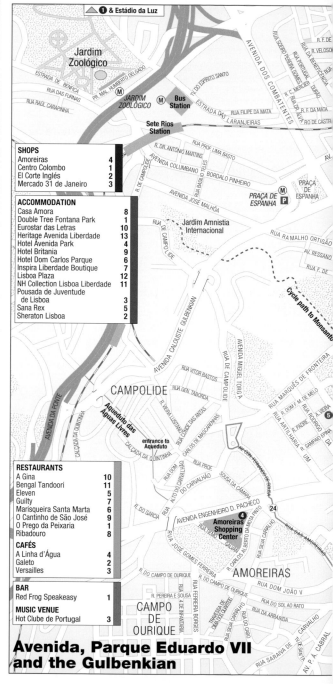

▲ ❶ & Estádio da Luz

Jardim Zoológico

ESTRADA DE BENFICA
PR. MAL. HUMBERTO DELGADO
RUA DAS FURNAS
RUA RAÚL CARAPINHA

Ⓜ JARDIM ZOOLÓGICO
Ⓜ Bus Station
Sete Rios Station

AVENIDA DOS COMBATENTES
TV. DO ESPÍRITO SANTO
ESTRADA DAS LARANJEIRAS
RUA FILIPE DA MATA
RUA SIDÓNIO PEREIRA
AVENIDA DO PORTUGAL
RUA DA BENEFICÊNCIA
RUA MERCIER
RUA DEL RUA
RUA DURÃO
R. F. DE
R. F. DA MATA
RO. DE CASTR
R. F. DE VELOSO

RUA PROF. LIMA BASTO
R. DR. ANTÓNIO MARTINS
AVENIDA COLUMBANO BORDALO PINHEIRO
RUA BASÍLIO TELES
AVENIDA JOSÉ MALHÓA

R. DE CAMPOLIDE

PRAÇA DE ESPANHA
Ⓜ Ⓟ
PRAÇA DE ESPANHA
AV.

SHOPS

Amoreiras	4
Centro Colombo	1
El Corte Inglés	2
Mercado 31 de Janeiro	3

ACCOMMODATION

Casa Amora	8
Double Tree Fontana Park	1
Eurostar das Letras	10
Heritage Avenida Liberdade	13
Hotel Avenida Park	4
Hotel Britania	9
Hotel Dom Carlos Parque	6
Inspira Liberdade Boutique	7
Lisboa Plaza	12
NH Collection Lisboa Liberdade	11
Pousada de Juventude de Lisboa	3
Sana Rex	5
Sheraton Lisboa	2

Jardim Amnistia Internacional

RUA DE CAMPOLIDE

RUA RAMALHO ORTIGÃO
AV. RESSANO
RUA F. DE

Cycle path to Monsant

AVENIDA CALOUSTE GULBENKIAN
RUA VÍTOR BASTOS
RUA DE CAMPOLIDE
RUA GEN. TABORDA
R. VIEIRA LUSITANO
R. CONDE DAS ANTAS
CARLOS DE MASCARENHAS

AVENIDA MIGUEL TORGA
RUA MARQUÊS DE FRONTEIRA
RUA DOM F. M. DE MELO
RUA ARTILHARIA R. UM
R. PADRE RODRIGO DA
R. SAMPAIO EPINA
❺

CAMPOLIDE

Aqueduto das Águas Livres
entrance to Aqueduto
CALÇADA DA QUINTINHA

AVENIDA DA PONTE
CALÇADA DA QUINTINHA

RUA DOM
ALTO DO CARVALHÃO
RUA PROF.
SOUSA DA CÂMARA

AVENIDA ENGENHEIRO D. PACHECO

R. DO GARCIA
R. DO CARVALHÃO

Amoreiras Shopping Center ❹
24

R. CARLOS ALBERTO DA MOTA PINTO
RUA SILVA CARVALHO
RUA DAS AMOREIRAS

RESTAURANTS

A Gina	10
Bengal Tandoori	11
Eleven	5
Guilty	7
Marisqueira Santa Marta	6
O Cantinho de São José	9
O Prego da Peixaria	1
Ribadouro	8

CAFÉS

A Linha d'Água	4
Galeto	2
Versailles	3

BAR

Red Frog Speakeasy	1

MUSIC VENUE

Hot Clube de Portugal	3

RUA JOSÉ GOMES FERREIRA
R. DO CAMPO DE OURIQUE
R. DO CAMPO DE OURIQUE
RUA DOM JOÃO V
RUA DO SOL AO RATO

AMOREIRAS

R. PEREIRA E SOUSA
RUA FERREIRA BORGES
4 DE INFANTARIA
RUA DA ARRÁBIDA
CARVALHO

CAMPO DE OURIQUE

TRAVESSA DE DIAS QUARTEIS
RUA SILVA CARVALHO
RUA DO CABO
RUA SARAIVA DE
TV. DE SANTO
AV. P. A. CABRAL

Avenida, Parque Eduardo VII and the Gulbenkian

Ernst, with both of whom she was good friends. Szenes and Vieira da Silva married in 1930 and, in 1936, both exhibited in Lisbon, where they briefly lived, before eventually settling in France. The foundation shows the development of the artists' works, with Vieira da Silva's more abstract, subdued paintings contrasting with flamboyant Szenes, some of whose paintings show the obvious influence of Miró.

Aqueduto das Águas Livres

MAP P.92, POCKET MAP F4
Entrance on Calçada da Quintinha 6, bus #712/#758 from Amoreiras ☎ 218 100 215, charge.

The towering aqueduct was opened in 1748, bringing a reliable source of safe fresh water to the city for the first time. Stretching for 60km (most of it underground), the aqueduct stood firm during the 1755 earthquake, though it later gained a more notorious reputation thanks to one Diogo Alves, a nineteenth-century serial killer who threw his victims off the top – a 70-metre drop. It is possible to walk across a 1.5km section of the aqueduct, though you'll need a head for heights. The walkable section is accessed off a quiet residential street through a small park in Campolide, 1km north of Praça das Amoreiras.

Fundação Calouste Gulbenkian

MAP P.92, POCKET MAP H2
Avda de Berna 45a Ⓦ gulbenkian.pt.

Set in extensive grounds, the foundation was set up by the Armenian oil magnate Calouste Gulbenkian (see page 95) whose legendary art-market coups included the acquisition of works from the Hermitage in St Petersburg. Today the Gulbenkian Foundation has a multi-million-dollar budget sufficient to finance work in all spheres of Portuguese cultural life. In this low-rise 1960s complex alone, it runs an orchestra, three concert halls and an attractive open-air amphitheatre.

Lalique jewellry, Museu Calouste Gulbenkian

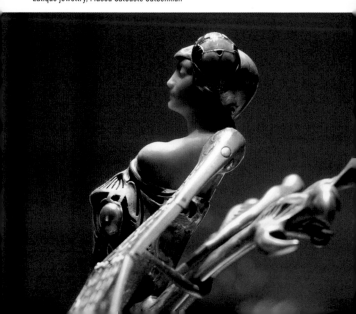

Calouste Gulbenkian

Calouste Sarkis Gulbenkian (1869–1955) was the Roman Abramovich of his era, making his millions from oil, but investing in the world's best art rather than footballers. Born of wealthy Armenian parents in Istanbul in 1869, he followed his father into the oil industry and eventually moved to England. After the Russian Revolution of 1917 he bought works from the Leningrad Hermitage. During World War II, his Turkish background made him unwelcome in Britain and Gulbenkian auctioned himself to whoever would have him. Portugal bid an aristocratic palace (a marquês was asked to move out) and tax exemption, to acquire one of the most important cultural patrons of the century. From 1942 to his death in 1955, he accumulated one of the best private art collections in the world. His dying wish was that all of his collection should be displayed in one place, and this was granted in 1969 with the opening of the Museu Calouste Gulbenkian.

Museu Calouste Gulbenkian: Founders Collection

MAP P.92, POCKET MAP H2

Avda de Berna 45a ⓦ gulbenkian.pt, charge (combined ticket available with Modern Art Collection), free Sun 2–6pm.

The **Museu Calouste Gulbenkian** combines the Founders Collection and the Modern Collection. The **Founders Collection** covers virtually every phase of Eastern and Western art. The small Egyptian room displays art from the Old Kingdom (c.2700 BC) up to the Roman period. Fine Roman statues, silver and glass, and gold jewellery from ancient Greece follow. The Islamic arts are magnificently represented by a variety of ornamental texts, opulently woven carpets, glassware and Turkish tiles. There is also porcelain from China, and beautiful Japanese prints and lacquerwork.

European art includes work from all the major schools. The seventeenth-century collection yields Peter Paul Rubens' graphic *The Love of the Centaurs* (1635) and Rembrandt's *Figure of an Old Man*. Featured eighteenth-century works include those by Jean-Honoré Fragonard and Thomas Gainsborough – in particular the stunning *Portrait of Mrs Lowndes-Stone*. The big names of nineteenth- to twentieth-century France – Manet, Monet, Degas, Millet and Renoir – are all represented, along with John Sargent and Turner's vivid *Wreck of a Transport Ship* (1810). Elsewhere you'll find Sèvres porcelain and furniture from the reigns of Louis XV and Louis XVI. The last room features an amazing collection of Art Nouveau jewellery by René Lalique. Don't miss the fantastical *Peitoral-libélula* (Dragonfly breastpiece) brooch, decorated with enamelwork, gold and diamonds.

Museu Calouste Gulbenkian: Modern Art Collection

MAP P.92, POCKET MAP H2

Main entrance on Rua Dr Nicolau de Bettencourt ⓦ gulbenkian.pt, charge (combined ticket available with Founders Collection), free Sun 2–6pm.

Although closed at the time of writing for renovation (check website for re-opening dates), the impressive **Modern Art Collection**,

Parque Eduardo VII

part of the Gulbenkian foundation (see page 94), features pop art, installations and sculptures – some witty, some baffling, but all thought-provoking. Most of the big names on the twentieth-century Portuguese scene are included, including portraits and sketches by José de Almada Negreiros (1873–1970), the founder of modernismo; the bright Futurist colours of Amadeo de Souza Cardoso; and works by Paula Rego, one of Portugal's leading contemporary artists, whose *Mãe* (1997) is outstanding. Pieces from major international artists such as David Hockney and Antony Gormley also feature.

Parque Eduardo VII

MAP P.92, POCKET MAP H4

The steep, formally laid out **Parque Eduardo VII** was named to honour Britain's King Edward VII when he visited the city in 1903. Its main building is the ornately tiled Pavilhão Carlos Lopes, built for the International Exhibition of Rio de Janeiro in 1922, then dismantled and rebuilt here in 1932; today, its hosts events and exhibitions such as the annual Moda Lisboa fashion week. North of here is the main viewing platform which offers commanding vistas of the city as well as Ferris wheel during the summer months. Another highlight if you have children is the superb Parque Infantil (free), a play area built round a mock galleon.

Two huge, rambling **estufas** (Ⓦestufafria.cm-lisboa.pt, charge) lie close by. Set in substantial former basalt quarries, both are filled with tropical plants, pools and endless varieties of palm and cactus. Of the two, the Estufa Quente (the hothouse) has the more exotic plants; the Estufa Fria (the coldhouse) hosts concerts and exhibitions.

Finally, the hilly northern reaches of the park contain an olive grove and a shallow lake which kids splash about in during the heat of the day.

Casa Museu Dr Anastácio Gonçalves

MAP P.92, POCKET MAP J3
Avda 5 de Outobro 6–8. Entrance on Rua Pinheiro Chagas Ⓦ bit.ly/MuseuGoncalves, charge.

This appealing neo-Romantic building with Art Nouveau touches – including a beautiful stained-glass window – was originally built for painter José Malhoa in 1904, but now holds the exquisite **private collection** of ophthalmologist Dr Anastácio Gonçalves, who bought the house in the 1930s. Highlights include paintings by Portuguese landscape artist João Vaz and by Malhoa himself, who specialized in historical paintings – his *Dream of Infante Henriques* is a typical example. You'll also find Chinese porcelain from the sixteenth-century Ming dynasty, along with furniture from England, France, Holland and Spain dating from the seventeenth century.

Praça de Touros

MAP P.92, POCKET MAP J1
Campo Pequeno
Ⓦ www.campopequeno.com.

Built in 1892, and substantially renovated in 2000 – with a retractable roof – the **Praça de Touros** at Campo Pequeno was built as an impressive Moorish-style bullring seating nine thousand spectators. Although the Portuguese claim their bullfighting is more humane than the Spanish equivalent as the bull isn't killed in the ring, the animal is usually injured and slaughtered later in any case, and performances have become more controversial in recent years. A few bullfights are still held each year, but attendance is not recommended. Surrounded by a ring of lively cafés and restaurants, the bullring also hosts concerts, live acts, musicals and other events. Beneath the arena is a surprisingly large underground shopping and cinema complex and a parking lot.

Jardim Zoológico

MAP P.92, POCKET MAP E1
Praça Marechal Humberto Delgado
Ⓦ www.zoo.pt, charge.

Lisbon's **Jardim Zoológico** was opened in 1884 and makes for an enjoyable excursion. There's a café-lined park area which you can visit for free and see monkeys, crocodiles and parrots. Once inside the zoo proper, a small

AVENIDA, PARQUE EDUARDO VII AND THE GULBENKIAN

Ethnic Lisbon

In the fifteenth century hundreds of Africans came to Lisbon on slave ships during Portugal's ruthless maritime explorations. Today, over 120,000 people of African and Asian descent live in the Greater Lisbon area, most hailing originally from Portugal's former colonies – Cape Verde, Angola, Mozambique, Brazil, Goa and Macao. The 1974 revolution and subsequent independence of the former colonies saw another wave of immigrants settle in the capital. Nowadays African and Brazilian culture permeates Lisbon life, influencing its music, food, television and street slang. Most Lisboetas are rightly proud of their cosmopolitan city, although, inevitably, racism persists and few from ethnic minorities have managed to break through the glass ceiling to the top jobs.

Jardim Zoológico

cable car (free) transports you over many of the animals, and there's a well-stocked reptile house and feeding sessions for sea lions and pelicans.

Estádio da Luz

MAP P.92, POCKET MAP H1
Ⓦ slbenfica.pt.

One of the most famous stadia in the world, the **Estádio da Luz** was built for and hosted the final of Euro 2004, when Portugal lost in a shock defeat to Greece. This is the home to Benfica (officially called Sport Lisboa e Benfica), the giant of Portuguese football who win (together with Porto) most domestic trophies. It's usually easy to buy match tickets from the stadium ticket office (from €25–50): expect to see the club mascot eagle flying across the pitch before the game starts. There is also an impressive **museum** (charge) with interactive exhibits tracing the club's prestigious history, including its two European Cup wins (1961 and 1962) and Europa League finals in 2013 and 2014.

Estádio José Alvalade

MAP P.92, POCKET MAP F1
Rua Professor Fernando da Fonseca, Apartado 4120 Ⓦ sporting.pt.

The impressive **José Alvalade Stadium** is home to Sporting Clube de Portugal, better known as Sporting Lisbon. Seating over 50,000 spectators, the stadium was built for Euro 2004 adjacent to the city's original football stadium. The team have pushed city rivals Benfica hard in recent years, and boast an impressive array of trophies: around 20 league wins (including 2021), 17 Portuguese Cup wins and a European Cup Winners Cup in 1964. Tickets for games (€20–45) are available at the stadium ticket office. You can also take a tour of the stadium and visit the museum (charge), which features the shirt of one of the club's best-known sons, Cristiano Ronaldo.

Shops

Amoreiras

MAP P.92, POCKET MAP F4

Avda Engenheiro Duarte Pacheco 2037. bus #758 from Cais de Sodré Ⓦ amoreiras.com.

Amoreiras, Lisbon's striking, postmodern commercial centre, is a wild fantasy of pink and blue towers sheltering ten cinemas, sixty cafés and restaurants, 250 shops, a hotel and a roof terrace with panoramic views over the city (Ⓦ amoreiras360view.com, charge). Built in 1985 and designed by adventurous Portuguese architect Tomás Taveira, most of its stores are open daily; Sunday sees the heaviest human traffic, with entire families descending for an afternoon out.

Centro Colombo

MAP P.92, POCKET MAP F1

Avda Lusíada Ⓜ Colégio Militar/Luz Ⓦ colombo.pt.

Iberia's largest shopping centre is almost a town in its own right, with over 340 shops, 60 restaurants and eight cinema screens. Major stores include Benfica's official store, C&A, Fnac, H&M, Levi's and Massimo Dutti.

El Corte Inglés

MAP P.92, POCKET MAP H3

Avda António Augusto de Aguiar 31 Ⓦ elcorteingles.pt.

A giant Spanish department store spread over nine floors, two of which are underground. The basement specializes in gourmet food, with various delis, bakers and a supermarket, while the upper floors offer a range of stylish goods, including clothes, sports gear, books and toys. The top floor packs in cafés and restaurants. There's also a fourteen-screen cinema in the basement (info on Ⓦ ucicinemas.pt).

Mercado 31 de Janeiro

MAP P.92, POCKET MAP J3

Rua Enginheiro Viera da Silva Ⓣ 218 160 970. Tues–Sat 7am–2pm.

This bustling local market is divided into sections; you'll find a colourful array of fresh fruit, vegetables, spices, fish, flowers and a few crafts.

Restaurants

A Gina

MAP P.92, POCKET MAP J5

Parque Mayer Ⓣ 213 420 296.

Tucked into the back of this historic theatre park, this traditional restaurant has been serving theatre goers and actors since the 1950s, and is well worth a visit for its big portions of tasty food. There's a large outdoor terrace, a cosy interior and a range of meat, fish and seafood dishes. Expect the likes of *pataniscas de bacalhau* (cod cakes) and generous salmon steaks, and don't miss the house dessert. €€

Bengal Tandoori

MAP P.92, POCKET MAP J5

Rua da Alegria 23 Ⓦ bengaltandoori.pt.

The decor might be Greco-Roman, but this is rated as one of the best Indian restaurants in town, up a steep side-street. Expect all the usual dishes – madras, biryanis and, of course, excellent tandoori – in an intimate space with good service. €€

Eleven

MAP P.92, POCKET MAP G3

Rua Marquês da Fronteira Ⓦ restauranteleven.com.

At the top of Parque Eduardo VII, this Michelin-starred restaurant, under the watchful eye of German head chef Joachim Koerper, hits the heights both literally and metaphorically. The interior is both intimate and bright, with wonderful city views. The food is expensive but not outrageous, with various tasting menus. Dishes include sea bass with chestnuts, suckling pig with passion fruit or mixed fish with mushrooms, and there's a fine wine list. €€€€

Guilty

MAP P.92, POCKET MAP H5
Rua Barata Salgueiro 28
Ⓦ restaurantesguilty.com.
Classy comfort foods are served (hence the name) in this modern diner, including pasta, carpaccio, giant pizzas and gourmet burgers from renowned chef Olivier. Just off the Avenida da Liberdade, it's a fashionable spot, too, with nighttime DJs. €€€

Marisqueira Santa Marta

MAP P.92, POCKET MAP J4
Trav do Enviato de Inglaterra 1 (off Rua de Santa Marta) Ⓣ 213 525 638.
Attractive and spacious *marisqueira* with bubbling tanks of crabs in one corner. Service is very attentive, and meals end with a complimentary port. €€

Eleven

O Cantinho de São José

MAP P.92, POCKET MAP J5
Rua São José 94 Ⓣ 213 427 866.
Friendly *tasca* serving good-value food – the menu is usually scrawled on a paper tablecloth outside. Dishes usually include grilled meat, salmon or other fish, with a fine house wine. €

O Prego da Peixaria

MAP P.92, POCKET MAP J1
Avenida da Igreja 34 77B
Ⓦ opregodapeixaria.com.
Traditional *pregos* are steak sandwiches, but this fashionable restaurant has embraced a whole host of varieties. As well as various versions of succulent steak, you can choose from the likes of *bacalhau*, tuna, mushroom or prawn; all are delicious if calorific. There are outdoor tables and brightly coloured murals on the walls inside. €€

Ribadouro

MAP P.92, POCKET MAP J5
Avda da Liberdade 155

W cervejariaribadouro.pt.
The Avenida's best *cervejaria*,
serving excellent seafood, including
the superb speciality prawns with
garlic and pricier lobster, crab,
oysters and clams – they also do a
decent *bacalhão* (salted cod) and
an excellent *gambas à bras* (prawns
with finely chipped potatoes). If
you don't fancy a full meal, take
a seat at the bar and order a beer
with a plate of prawns. It's best to
book for the restaurant, especially
at weekends. €€€

Cafés

A Linha d'Água
MAP P.92, POCKET MAP G3
Jardim Amália Rodrigues **T** 213 814 327.
Facing a small lake, this glass-
fronted café is at the northern end
of the park. It's a tranquil spot
to sip a coffee or beer, and serves
excellent value buffet lunches,
too, such as salted cod cakes with
salad. €

Galeto
MAP P.92, POCKET MAP J2
Avda da República 14 **T** 213 544 444.
Late-opening café with striking
1960s decor and an array of snacks,
pastries, beers and coffees. Drop in
for a full meal at sensible prices by
the bar. €€

Versailles
MAP P.92, POCKET MAP J2
Avda da República 15a **T** 213 546 340.
This traditional café, full of bustling
waiters, is busiest at around 4pm,
when Lisbon's elderly dames gather
for a chat beneath the chandeliers.
Drop in for tasty cakes and pastries,
coffee or a sandwich in traditional
surroundings. €

Bar

Red Frog Speakeasy
MAP P.92, POCKET MAP J5
Praça da Alegria 66b **T** 215 831 120.

Pastelaria Versailles

Taking inspiration from the
prohibition era in the US, this
upmarket cocktail bar has a
secretive air, enhanced by the fact
you have to ring a bell to enter
(look for the red frog on the
wall). Many of the best cocktails
are made from local Portuguese
brandies, *ginginha* and herbal
liqueurs: try the Mr Brown,
spiked with gin and Madeira wine
and mixed with Earl Grey tea,
rhubarb and bergamot.

Music venue

Hot Clube de Portugal
MAP P.92, POCKET MAP J5
Praça da Alegria 48 **W** hcp.pt.
Dating from 1948 – making it
one of Europe's oldest jazz clubs –
this tiny basement club hosts top
names in the jazz world, along with
a range of local performers. The
venue was largely rebuilt after a
recent fire.

Parque das Nações

The Parque das Nações (pronounced "na-soysh"), or "Park of Nations", is the high-tech former site of Expo '98. Its flat, pedestrianized walkways, lined with fountains and futuristic buildings, are in complete contrast to the narrow, precipitous streets of old Lisbon, and it is packed with locals on summer weekends. The main highlight is the giant Oceanário de Lisboa, but it also features a casino, a cable car, riverside walkways, a giant park and two of Lisbon's largest concert venues. It is also impossible to miss the astonishing 17km-long Vasco da Gama bridge over the Tejo. Constructed in time for the Expo in 1998, it is still the longest bridge in Western Europe.

Olivais dock and the Altice Arena

MAP P.104, POCKET MAP B17–18

The central focus of the Parque das Nações is the Olivais dock, overlooked by pixie-hatted twin towers, and where boats pull in on Tejo cruises. The dock's **Marina** (☏ 218 949 066) offers canoeing and sailing lessons and riverboat tours. The main building facing the dock is the Pavilhão de Portugal (Portugal Pavilion), a multipurpose arena designed by Álvaro Siza Vieira, architect of the reconstructed Chiado district, featuring an enormous, sagging concrete canopy on its south side. It now hosts temporary exhibitions. Opposite here – past Antony Gormley's weird *Rhizome* sculpture, a tree of cast-iron legs – is the spaceship-like **Altice Arena** (Ⓦ arena.altice.pt), Portugal's largest indoor arena and the venue for major visiting bands (including Justin Bieber, Coldplay and Madonna) and sporting events. It also hosted the 2005 MTV Europe Music Awards and the Eurovision Song Contest 2018.

Pavilhão do Conhecimento (Ciência Viva)

MAP P.104, POCKET MAP B18
Alameda dos Oceanos
Ⓦ pavconhecimento.pt, charge.

Run by Portugal's Ministry of Science and Technology, the **Knowledge Pavilion** (Live Science) hosts excellent changing exhibitions on subjects like 3D animation and the latest computer technology, and is usually bustling

Visiting the park

The best way to reach the park is to take the metro to Oriente or bus #728 from Praça do Comércio. Oriente metro station exits in the bowels of the Estação do Oriente, a cavernous glass and concrete station designed by Spanish architect Santiago Calatrava.

The park's website (Ⓦ portaldasnacoes.pt) has details of the day's events, and details of the urban art dotted round the area, from murals and graffiti art to statues and sculptures.

Waterfall in the Jardins da Água, Parque das Nações

with school parties. The permanent interactive exhibits – allowing you to create a vortex in water or a film of detergent the size of a baby's blanket – are particularly good, and there's also a cybercafé offering free internet.

Jardins da Água

MAP P.104, POCKET MAP B19

The **Jardins da Água** (Water Gardens), crisscrossed by waterways and ponds, are based on the stages of a river's drainage pattern, from stream to estuary. They are not huge, but linked by stepping stones, and there are enough gushing fountains, water gadgets and pumps to keep children occupied for hours.

Oceanário

MAP P.104, POCKET MAP B18

Esplanada Dom Carlos I Ⓦ oceanario.pt, charge.

Designed by Peter Chermayeff and looking like something off the set of a James Bond film, Lisbon's

Oceanário (Oceanarium) is one of Europe's largest and contains some 8,000 fish and marine animals. Its main feature is the enormous central tank which you can look into from different levels for close-up views of circling sharks down to the rays burying themselves in the sand. Almost more impressive though, are the re-creations of various ocean ecosystems, such as the Antarctic tank, containing frolicking penguins, and the Pacific tank, where otters bob about in the rock pools. On a darkened lower level, smaller tanks contain shoals of brightly coloured tropical fish and other warm-water creatures. Find a window free of school parties and the whole experience becomes the closest you'll get to deep-sea diving without getting wet.

The Teleférico and the Jardins Garcia da Orta

MAP P.104, POCKET MAP B16–18

Ⓦ telecabinelisboa.pt, charge.

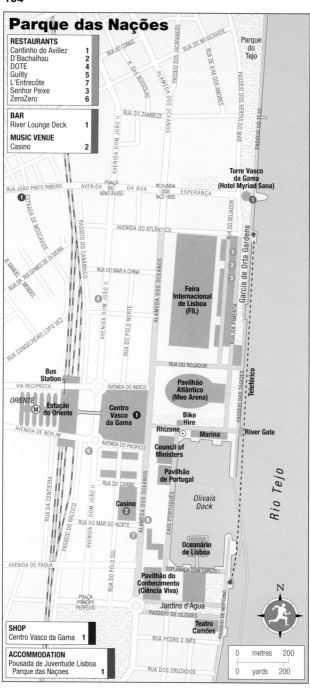

Parque das Nações

RESTAURANTS
Cantinho do Avillez 1
D'Bachalhau 2
DOTE 4
Guilty 5
L'Entrecôte 7
Senhor Peixe 3
ZeroZero 6

BAR
River Lounge Deck 1

MUSIC VENUE
Casino 2

SHOP
Centro Vasco da Gama 1

ACCOMMODATION
Pousada de Juventude Lisboa
Parque das Nações 1

The ski-lift-style *teleférico* (cable car) rises up to 20m as it shuttles you over Olivais docks to the northern side of the Parque, giving commanding views over the site on the way. It drops down to the **Garcia da Orta gardens**, containing exotic trees from Portugal's former colonies. Behind the gardens, Rua Pimenta is lined with a motley collection of international restaurants, from Irish to Israeli.

Torre Vasco da Gama

MAP P.104, POCKET MAP B16
Cais das Naus Ⓦ myriad.pt.

Once an integral part of an oil refinery, the **Torre Vasco da Gama** (Vasco da Gama Tower) is, at 145m high, Lisbon's tallest structure. The tower is now integrated into the five-star hotel *Myriad by Sana*, Lisbon's answer to Dubai's *Burj Al Arab*.

Torre Vasco da Gama

Parque do Tejo

MAP P.104, POCKET MAP B15

Unfurling along the waterfront for 2km right up to the Vasco da Gama bridge, **Parque do Tejo** is threaded through with bike trails and riverside walks. It's also a great spot for a picnic – supplies are available in the Vasco da Gama shopping centre.

Feira Internacional de Lisboa

MAP P.104, POCKET MAP B16–17
Rua do Bojador Ⓦ www.fil.pt.

Lisbon's trade fair hall, the **Feira Internacional de Lisboa** (FIL), hosts various events, including a handicrafts fair displaying ceramics and crafts from around the country (usually in July).

Vasco da Gama

The opening of Parque das Nações in 1998 celebrated the 500th anniversary of Vasco da Gama's arrival in India. One of Portugal's greatest explorers, Da Gama was born in Sines in 1460. By the 1490s he was working for João II, protecting trading stations along the African coast. This persuaded the next king, Manuel I, to commission him to find a sea route to India. He departed Lisbon in July 1497 with a fleet of four ships, reaching southern Africa in December. The following May they finally reached Calicut in southwest India, obtaining trading terms before departing in August 1498. The return voyage took a full year, by which time Da Gama had lost two of his ships and half his men. But he was richly rewarded by the king, his voyage inspiring Camões to write *Os Lusiadas*, Portugal's most famous epic poem. Da Gama returned to India twice more, the final time in 1524 when he contracted malaria and died in the town of Cochin.

Shop

Centro Vasco da Gama

MAP P.104, POCKET MAP B17
Avda D. João II 40 Ⓦ centrovascodagama.pt.
Three floors of local and
international stores are housed
beneath a glass roof washed by
permanently running water;
international branches include
Zara, Calvin Klein, Timberland
and Mango, while local sports
and bookshops also feature. There
are plenty of fast-food outlets
and good-value restaurants on
the top floor, six cinema screens,
children's areas and a Continente
supermarket on the lower floor.

Restaurants

Cantinho do Avillez

MAP P.104, POCKET MAP C13
Rua Bojador 55 Ⓦ cantinhodoavillez.pt.
The top place to eat in the
Parque das Nações, this bright
contemporary restaurant opens
onto a great outdoor terrace
and serves sublime food by José
Avillez. The menu features his

trademark Portuguese dishes
with a twist, such as cod with
exploding olives, Algarvian shrimp
with Thai sauce and hamburger
with foie gras. €€€

D'Bacalhau

MAP P.104, POCKET MAP B16
Rua do Pimenta 43–45
Ⓦ restaurantebacalhau.com.
If you want to sample one of the
alleged 365 recipes for *bacalhau* –
salted cod – this is a good place to
come, as it serves quite a range of
them: *bacalhau com natas* (with a
creamy sauce) is always good. There
are also other dishes, including a
selection of fresh fish and meat
dishes. €€

DOTE

MAP P.104, POCKET MAP A17
Avenida Dom João II 43E 77B ☎ 215 838
946, Ⓦ dote.pt. Daily noon–1am.
This modern space serves
reasonably-priced specialities
from Portugal's second city, Porto,
including its famed *franceshinhas*,
an OTT version of France's *croque
monsieur* with additional toppings.
Other dishes include tuna *pregos* (in
a bun), soups and salads. €€

Cantinho do Avillez

Casino

Guilty

MAP P.104, POCKET MAP A18
Avenida Dom João II 27 77b
Ⓦ restaurantesguilty.com.
Classy and affordable comfort foods
from leading chef Olivier da Costa,
including giant pizzas, burgers,
various pasta dishes and cocktails.
There's also a special Sport TV area
where you can dine and watch live
sports events (mostly football). €€

L'Entrecôte

MAP P.104, POCKET MAP B18
Alameda dos Oceanos 1.02.12a
Ⓦ brasserieentrecote.pt.
Local branch of the Lisbon
restaurant famed for its fabulous
steaks cooked with sublime sauces
– choose from various menus. €€€

Senhor Peixe

MAP P.104, POCKET MAP B16
Rua da Pimenta 35–37 Ⓣ 218 955 892.
"Mr Fish" is widely thought to
serve up some of the best fresh
seafood in the Lisbon region –
check the counter for the day's
catch or choose a lobster from the
bubbling tank. Most dishes are
grilled in the open kitchen. There's
also a little fish-themed bar and
pleasant outdoor tables. €€

ZeroZero

MAP P.104, POCKET MAP B18
Alameda dos Oceanos, Lote 2
Ⓦ pizzeriazerozero.pt.
This classy pizza restaurant uses
Italian ingredients for its tasty
pizzas and also serves a range of
pastas, salads and quality antipasti.
There's also a bar serving prosecco
and cocktails, plus an outside
terrace with river views. €€

Bar

River Lounge Deck

MAP P.104, POCKET MAP B16
Myriad by Sana, Cais das Naus, Lote
2.23.01 Ⓦ myriad.pt.
Inside the deluxe *Myriad by
Sana* hotel, the ultra-hip *River
Lounge Deck* juts into the Tejo
so you feel as if you're right on
the water. Cocktails and drinks
are predictably expensive, but it's
worth it for the view. Frequent live
music after 7pm.

Music venue

Casino

MAP P.104, POCKET MAP A18
Alameda dos Oceanos 45 Ⓦ casino-lisboa.pt.
Opened in 2006, this state-of-the-
art space – with its glass-cylinder
entrance hall – hosts top shows
from Broadway and London
as well as major concerts in the
performance hall, which has a
retractable roof. The usual casino
attractions also feature.

Sintra

If you make just one day-trip from Lisbon, choose the beautiful hilltop town of Sintra, the former summer residence of Portuguese royalty and a UNESCO World Heritage Site since 1995. Not only does the town boast two of Portugal's most extraordinary palaces, it also contains a semitropical garden, a Moorish castle and proximity to some great beaches. Looping around a series of wooded ravines and with a climate that encourages moss and ferns to grow from every nook and cranny, Sintra consists of three districts: Sintra-Vila, with most of the historical attractions; Estefânia, a ten-minute walk to the east, where trains from Lisbon pull in; and São Pedro to the south, well known for its antique shops and best visited on the eve of São Pedro (June 28–29), the main saint's day, and for its market on the second and fourth Sunday of the month.

Sintra-Vila

MAP P.110

The historic centre of Sintra spreads across the slopes of several steep hills, themselves loomed over by wooded heights topped by the Moorish castle and the Palácio da Pena. Dominating the centre of **Sintra-Vila** are the tapering chimneys of the Palácio Nacional, surrounded by an array of tall houses painted in the prettiest pale pink, ochre or mellow yellow tones, many with ornate turrets and decorative balconies peering out to the plains of Lisbon far below. All this is highly scenic – though, in fact, Sintra looks at its best seen on the way in from the station. Summer crowds can swamp the narrow central streets, and once you've seen the sights, you're best

Visiting Sintra

There are trains from Lisbon's Rossio station (every 10–30min; 45min; €2.30 single). A land train (6 daily; €10) runs from near Sintra station in a circuit via the Palácio Nacional, the Moorish Castle, the Pena Palace and the Quinta da Regaleira. Alternatively, bus #434 takes a circular route from Sintra station to most of the sites mentioned in this chapter (every 20–40min from 9.30am–6.20pm; €7.60) and allows you to get on and off whenever you like on the circuit. Also useful is bus #435 which runs from Sintra station to Monserrate gardens via Sintra-Vila and Quinta da Regaleira (every 45min 9.40am–6.15pm; €5.50 return). To see the area around Sintra, including the coast, consider a Day-rover (Turístico Diário) ticket on the local Scotturb buses (ⓦscotturb.com; €15). Ask at the tourist office about various combined tickets that can save money on entry to the main sites.

Palácio Nacional

off heading out of town to the see the surrounding attractions up in the hills.

Palácio Nacional

MAP P.110
Largo da Rainha Dona Amélia
Ⓦ **parquesdesintra.pt, charge.**
Best seen early or late in the day to avoid the crowds, the sumptuous **Palácio Nacional** was probably already in existence at the time of the Moors. It takes its present form from the rebuilding of Dom João I (1385–1433) and his successor, Dom Manuel I, the chief royal beneficiary of Vasco da Gama's explorations. Its exterior style is an amalgam of Gothic – featuring impressive battlements – and Manueline, tempered inside by a good deal of Moorish influence. Sadly, after the fall of the monarchy in 1910, most of the surrounding walls and medieval houses were destroyed. Highlights on the lower floor include the Manueline **Sala dos Cisnes**, so-called for the swans (*cisnes*) on its ceiling, and the Sala das Pegas, which takes its name from the flock of magpies (*pegas*)

painted on the frieze and ceiling – João I, caught in the act of kissing a lady-in-waiting by his queen, reputedly had the room decorated with as many magpies as there were women at court, to imply they were all magpie-like gossips.

Best of the upper floor is the gallery above the palace chapel. Beyond, a succession of **state rooms** finishes with the Sala das Brasões, its domed and coffered ceiling emblazoned with the arms of 72 noble families. Finally, don't miss the kitchens, whose roofs taper into the giant chimneys that are the palace's distinguishing features. The Palace also hosts events for the Sintra Music Festival (see page 142).

MU.SA – Museu das Artes de Sintra

MAP P.110
Avda Heliodoro Salgado Ⓦ **bit.ly/MUSA-Sintra, free.**
Inside Sintra's beautiful former casino, this appealing contemporary **art museum** is dedicated to important Portuguese artists such as Emílio de Paula Campos (1884–1943), who

SINTRA

Sintra

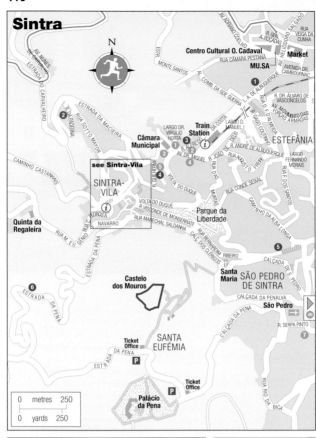

Centro Cultural O. Cadaval
Market
RUA CÂMARA PESTANA
MU.SA
ESTEFÂNIA
Câmara Municipal
Train Station
LARGO DR. VIRGÍLIO HORTA
see Sintra-Vila
SINTRA-VILA
Parque da Liberdade
Quinta da Regaleira
VOLTA DO DUQUE
RUA VISCONDE DE MONSERRATE
RUA MARECHAL SALDANHA
Santa Maria
SÃO PEDRO DE SINTRA
Castelo dos Mouros
São Pedro
Ticket Office
SANTA EUFÉMIA
Ticket Office
Palácio da Pena

0   metres   250
0   yards   250

Sintra-Vila

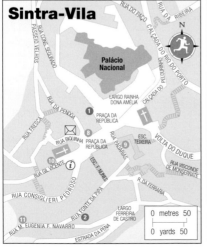

Palácio Nacional
LARGO RAINHA DONA AMÉLIA
PRAÇA DA REPÚBLICA
PRAÇA DA REPÚBLICA
VOLTA DO DUQUE
RUA VISCONDE DE MONSERRATE
LARGO FERREIRA DE CASTRO

0   metres   50
0   yards   50

ACCOMMODATION

Casa do Valle	2
Chalet Relogio	6
Chalet Saudade	3
Hotel Nova Sintra	1
Hotel Sintra Jardim	5
Moon Hill Hostel	4

RESTAURANTS

A Tasca da Paula	3
Cantinho de São Pedro	7
Harko's	6
Incomum	2
Páteo do Garrett	11
Restaurante Regional de Sintra	1
Tulhas	10

CAFÉS

Adega das Caves	8
Casa Piriquita	9
Fábrica das Verdadeiras Queijadas da Sapa	5
Café Saudade	4

BARS

Bar Fonte da Pipa	2
Café Paris	1

Castelo dos Mouros

portrays traditional rural scenes, and innovative sculptress Dorita Castel-Branco (1936–1996). There is also a photography room and temporary exhibits (charge).

Quinta da Regaleira

MAP P.110
Rua Barbosa do Bocage Ⓦ regaleira.pt, charge.

The **Quinta da Regaleira** is one of Sintra's most elaborate estates. It was designed at the end of the nineteenth century by Italian architect and theatre set designer Luigi Manini for wealthy Brazilian merchant António Augusto Carvalho Monteiro. Manini's penchant for the dramatic is obvious: the principal building, the mock-Manueline **Palácio dos Milhões**, sprouts turrets and towers, while the interior boasts Art Nouveau tiles and elaborate Rococo wooden ceilings.

The surrounding **gardens** shelter fountains, terraces and grottoes, with the highlight being the Initiation Well, inspired by the initiation practices of the Freemasons. Entering via a Harry Potter-esque revolving stone door, you walk down a moss-covered spiral staircase to the foot of the well and through a tunnel, which eventually resurfaces at the edge of a lake (though in winter you exit from a shorter tunnel so as not to disturb a colony of hibernating bats).

In summer, the gardens host occasional performances of live music, usually classical or jazz, and light shows.

Castelo dos Mouros

MAP P.110
Ⓦ parquesdesintra.pt, charge.

Reached on bus #434 or a steep drive, the ruined ramparts of the **Castelo dos Mouros** are truly spectacular. It's also a pleasant, if steep, walk up (30–40min): start at the Calçada dos Clérigos, near the church of Santa Maria, where a stone pathway leads all the way up to the lower slopes, where you can see a Moorish grain silo and a ruined twelfth-century church. To enter the castle itself, you'll need to buy a ticket from the road exit. Built in the ninth century, the castle was taken from the Moors

Palácio da Pena

in 1147 by Afonso Henriques, Portugal's first monarch: the ruins of a Moorish mosque remain. The castle walls were allowed to fall into disrepair over subsequent centuries, though they were restored in the mid-nineteenth century under the orders of Ferdinand II. The castle is partly built into two craggy pinnacles, and views from up here are dazzling both inland and across to the Atlantic. Recent excavations have revealed the ruins of Muslim houses, thirty medieval Christian graves and ceramic vases dating back to the fifth century BC.

Palácio da Pena

MAP P.110
Estrada da Pena ⓦ parquedesintra.pt, charge.

Bus #434 stops opposite the lower entrance to Parque da Pena, a stretch of rambling woodland with a scattering of lakes and follies. At the top of the park, about twenty minutes' walk from the entrance or a short ride on a shuttle bus (charge), looms the fabulous **Palácio da Pena**, a wild fantasy of domes, towers, ramparts and walkways, approached through mock-Manueline gateways and a drawbridge that does not draw. A compelling riot of kitsch, the palace was built in the 1840s to the specifications of Ferdinand of Saxe-Coburg-Gotha, husband of Queen Maria II, with the help of the German architect Baron Eschwege. The interior is preserved exactly as it was left by the royal family when they fled Portugal in 1910. The result is fascinating: rooms of stone

Visiting Praia das Maçãs

Quaint old trams shuttle from near the Centro Cultural Olga Cadaval to the coastal resort of Praia das Maçãs via Colares (June–Sept 10.20am–5pm daily; 40min; €3 single). However, check the latest routes and timetables in the Sintra tourist office or on ☎ 219 238 766, as there are frequent shortenings of the route or alterations to the service.

decorated to look like wood, statues of turbaned Moors nonchalantly holding electric chandeliers – it's all here. Of an original convent, founded in the early sixteenth century to celebrate the first sight of Vasco da Gama's returning fleet, only a beautiful, tiled chapel and Manueline cloister have been retained.

You can also look round the mock-Alpine **Chalet Condessa d'Edla**, built by Ferdinand in the 1860s as a retreat for his second wife.

Monserrate

MAP P.113
Estrada da Monserrate Ⓦ parquedesintra. pt, charge.

The name most associated with the fabulous gardens and palace of **Monserrate** is that of William Beckford, the wealthiest untitled Englishman of his age, who rented the estate from 1793 to 1799, having been forced to flee

Britain after he was caught in a compromising position with a sixteen-year-old boy. Setting about improving the place, he landscaped a waterfall and even imported a flock of sheep from his estate.

Half a century later, a second immensely rich Englishman, Sir Francis Cook, bought the estate and imported the head gardener from Kew to lay out water plants, tropical ferns and palms, and just about every known conifer. For a time Monserrate boasted the only lawn in Iberia, and it remains one of Europe's most richly stocked gardens, with over a thousand different species of subtropical tree and plant.

From the entrance, paths lead steeply down through lush undergrowth to a ruined chapel, half engulfed by a giant banyan tree. From here, lawns take you up to Cook's main legacy, a great **Victorian palace** inspired by Brighton Pavilion, with its mix of

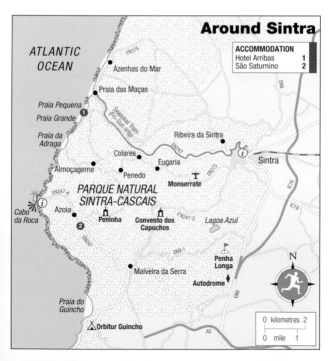

Around Sintra

ATLANTIC OCEAN

ACCOMMODATION	
Hotel Arribas	1
São Saturnino	2

Azenhas do Mar

Praia das Maças

Praia Pequena
Praia Grande

Praia da Adraga

Seasonal Tram (Fri–Sun only)

Ribeira da Sintra

Colares

Eugaria

Almoçageme

Penedo

Monserrate

Sintra

PARQUE NATURAL SINTRA-CASCAIS

Cabo da Roca

Azoia

Peninha

Convento dos Capuchos

Lagoa Azul

Penha Longa

Malveira da Serra

Autodromo

Praia do Guincho

Orbitur Guincho

N

0 kilometres 2
0 mile 1

Azenhas do Mar

Moorish and Italian decoration – the dome is modelled on the Duomo in Florence. The interior has been restored after years of neglect, and you can now admire the amazingly intricate plasterwork which covers almost every wall and ceiling. The park also has a decent café.

Azenhas do Mar

MAP P.113

Bus #441 from Sintra (every 1–2hr, 40min). Whitewashed cottages tumble down the steep cliff-face at the pretty village of **Azenhas do Mar**, one of the most lively villages of the Sintra coast. The beach is small, but there are man-made seawater pools for swimming in when the ocean is too rough.

Praia das Maçãs

MAP P.113

Bus #441 from Sintra (every 1–2hr; 30min); or Praia das Maçãs tram from Sintra.

The largest and liveliest resort on this coast, **Praia das Maçãs** is also the easiest to reach from Sintra – take the tram (see box, page 113) for the most enjoyable journey. Along with a big swath of sand, there's an array of bars and restaurants to suit all budgets.

Praia Grande

MAP P.113

Bus #441 from Sintra (every 1–2hr; 25min).

Set in a wide, sandy cliff-backed bay, this is one of the best and safest **beaches** on the Sintra coast, though its breakers attract surfers aplenty. In August the World Bodyboarding Championships are held here, along with games such as volleyball and beach rugby. Plenty of inexpensive cafés and restaurants are spread out along the beachside road, and if the sea gets too rough, there are giant sea pools (May–Oct, charge) on the approach to the beach.

Praia da Adraga

MAP P.113

No public transport; by car, follow the signs from the village of Almoçageme. **Praia da Adraga** was flatteringly voted one of Europe's best beaches by a British newspaper; the unspoilt, cliff-backed, sandy bay with just one beach restaurant is certainly far quieter than the other resorts, but it takes the full brunt of the Atlantic, so you'll need to take great care when swimming.

Cabo da Roca

MAP P.113
Bus #403 from Sintra or Cascais train stations (roughly hourly; 45min).
Little more than a windswept **rocky cape** with a lighthouse, this is the most westerly point in mainland Europe, which guarantees a steady stream of visitors – get there early to avoid the coach parties. You can soak up the views from the café-restaurant and handicraft shop, and buy a certificate to prove you've been here at the little tourist office (daily 9am–7.30pm, Oct–May until 6.30pm; ☎ 219 238 543).

Convento dos Capuchos

MAP P.113
No public transport, a return taxi from Sintra with a 1hr stopover costs around €40 ⓦ parquesdesintra.pt, charge.
If you have your own transport, don't miss a trip to the **Convento dos Capuchos**, an extraordinary hermitage with tiny, dwarf-like cells cut from the rock and lined with cork – hence its popular name of the Cork Convent. It was occupied for three hundred years until

being finally abandoned in 1834 by its seven remaining monks, who must have found the gloomy warren of rooms and corridors too much to maintain. Some rooms – the penitents' cells – can only be entered by crawling through 70cm-high doors; here, and on every other ceiling, doorframe and lintel, are attached panels of cork, taken from the surrounding woods. Elsewhere, you'll come across a washroom, kitchen, refectory, tiny chapels, and even a bread oven set apart from the main complex.

Peninha

MAP P.113
With your own transport, it is worth exploring the dramatic wooded landscape between Capuchos and Cabo da Roca, much of it studded with giant moss-covered boulders. Some 3km from Capuchos lies **Peninha**, a spectacularly sited hermitage perched on a granite crag. The sixteenth-century Baroque interior is usually locked, but climb up anyway to get dazzling views of the Sintra coast towards Cascais. You can also take a waymarked 4.5km trail round the crag; otherwise it is a short return walk from the woodland car park.

Convento dos Capuchos

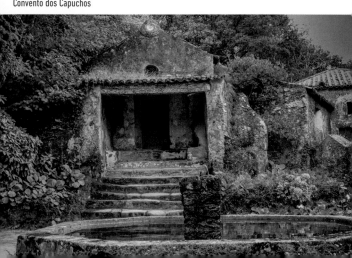

Restaurants

A Tasca da Paula

MAP P.110
Largo Dr. Virgílio Horta 5 Ⓦ bit.ly/
TascaPaula.
In total contrast to Sintra's
wonderfully ornate Town Hall
opposite, this is a simple but
recommended little *tasca* serving
traditional Portuguese food.
Squeeze onto a table for good-
value, no-nonsense fish, stews and
grills. €

Cantinho de São Pedro

MAP P.110
**Praça D. Fernando II 18, São Pedro de
Sintra** Ⓦ cantinhosaopedro.com.
Large restaurant with bare stone
walls overlooking an attractive
courtyard just off São Pedro's main
square. The traditional dishes (such
as *bacalhau com natas*) are better
than the international ones. On
cool evenings a log fire keeps things
cosy. €€

Harko's

MAP P.110
Rua Serpa Pinto 4, São Pedro de Sintra
Ⓦ harkos.pt.
Perhaps unusually for village-like
São Pedro, this is a top-notch
Japanese restaurant serving a tasty
range of sushi and sashimi. Local
ingredients feature, such as scallops
and fresh tuna, and there are also
good vegetarian options. €€€

Incomum

MAP P.110
Rua Dr. Alfredo Costa 22, Sintra
Ⓦ incomumbyluissantos.pt.
Close to the station, this upmarket
restaurant and wine bar is run by
chef Luís Santos. His stints in some
of Switzerland's top restaurants are
reflected in a menu featuring the
likes of scallops with mushroom
risotto, black linguini with seafood
and steak with sweet potatoes,
though the ingredients are local
and top quality. €€€

Páteo do Garrett

MAP P.110
Rua Maria Eugénia Reis F. Navarro 7
Ⓦ pateodogarrett.com.
Although this café-restaurant
has a dark, dim interior, it's also
got a lovely sunny patio offering
fine views over the village. Serves
mixed meat kebabs, monkfish rice
and the like, or just pop in for a
drink. €€

Restaurante Regional de Sintra

MAP P.110
Trav do Município 2 ☎ 219 234 444.
In a lovely old building next to the
Câmara Municipal, this traditional
and slightly formal restaurant
serves tasty dishes at reasonable
prices – fresh fish, grilled meats
and a very good *crêpe de marisco*
(seafood crêpe), as well as some fine
desserts, €€

Tulhas

MAP P.110
Rua Gil Vicente 4–6 ☎ 219 232 378.
Imaginative cooking in a fine
building converted from old grain
silos – the old grain well takes
pride of place in the floor. The
giant mixed grills for two will
keep carnivores happy, while the
weekend specials are usually good
value, with the usual range of
grilled meat and fish. €€

Cafés

Adega das Caves

MAP P.110
Rua da Pendoa 2–10 ☎ 219 230 848.
Bustling café-bar in the former
palace coal merchants, attracting a
predominantly local and youthful
clientele; the restaurant does good
value meals. €

Casa Piriquita

MAP P.110
Rua das Padarias 1 ☎ 219 230 626.
Cosy tearoom and bakery,
dating from 1862, which can

Café Paris

get busy with locals queueing to buy *queijadas de Sintra* (sweet cheesecakes), *travesseiros* (doughy almond cakes) and other pastries. €

Fábrica das Verdadeiras Queijadas da Sapa

MAP P.110
Volta do Duche 12 ⓘ 219 230 493.
This old-fashioned café is famed for its traditional *queijadas* (cheesecakes), made on the premises for over a century. It's a bit dingy inside, so it's best to buy takeaways to sustain you on your walk to the centre. €

Café Saudade

MAP P.110
Avda Dr. Miguel Bombarda 6, Sintra ⓘ 212 428 804.
This buzzy café used to be a factory selling *queijadas* and has a warren of rooms and its own art gallery, with occasional live music. As well as cakes, scones and sandwiches, it serves

some interesting *petiscos* such as Madeiran garlic bread and regional cheeses. A wide range of drinks and teas includes Gorreana tea from the Azores. €

Bars

Bar Fonte da Pipa

MAP P.110
Rua Fonte da Pipa 11–13 ⓘ 219 234 437.
Laid-back bar with low lighting, comfy chairs and a fine sangria. It's up the hill from *Casa Piriquita*, next to the lovely ornate fountain (*fonte*) that the street is named after.

Café Paris

MAP P.110
Praçe da República 32 ⓘ 219 232 375.
This attractive blue-tiled café-bar is the highest-profile in town, which means steep prices for not especially exciting food, although it is a great place for a cocktail.

The Lisbon coast

Lisbon's most accessible beaches lie along the Cascais coast just beyond the point where the Tejo flows into the Atlantic. Famed for its casino, Estoril has the best sands, though neighbouring Cascais has more buzz. The River Tejo separates Lisbon from high-rise Caparica, to the south, on a superb stretch of wave-pounded beach, popular with surfers.

Estoril

MAP P.120

With its grandiose villas, luxury hotels and health spa, **Estoril** (pronounced é-stril) has pretensions towards being a Portuguese Riviera. The centre is focused on the leafy **Parque do Estoril** and its enormous casino (semiformal attire required; ⓦcasino-estoril.pt, free). During World War II, this was where exiled royalty hung out and many spies made their names. Ian Fleming was based here to keep an eye on double agents, and used his experience at the casino as inspiration for the first James Bond novel, *Casino Royale*.

The resort's fine sandy beach, **Praia de Tamariz**, is backed by some ornate villas and a seafront promenade that stretches northwest to Cascais, a pleasant twenty-minute stroll. In summer, firework displays take place above the beach every Saturday at midnight.

Estoril is also famed for its world-class **golf courses** which lie a short distance inland (more information online at ⓦportugalgolf.pt); it also hosts the Estoril Open tennis tournament in April or May (ⓦmillenniumestorilopen.com).

Tamariz beach in Estoril

Transport to Estoril and Cascais

Trains from Lisbon's Cais do Sodré (every 15–30min; 35min to Estoril, 40min to Cascais; €2.85 single) wend along the shore. There are also regular buses to and from Sintra, or it's a fine drive down the corniche.

Cascais

MAP P.119

Cascais (pronounced cash-kaysh) is a highly attractive former fishing village, liveliest round Largo Luís de Camões, at one end of Rua Frederico Arouca, the main mosaic-paved pedestrian thoroughfare.

Praia da Conceição is the ideal beach to lounge on or try out a range of watersports. The rock-fringed smaller beaches of **Praia da Rainha** and **Praia da Ribeira** are off the central stretch, while regular buses run 6km northwest to **Praia do Guincho**, a fabulous sweep of surf-beaten sands.

Cascais is at its most charming in the grid of streets north of the **Igreja da Assunção** – its *azulejos* predate the earthquake of 1755. Nearby, on Rua Júlio Pereira de Melo, the engaging **Museu do Mar** (☎214 815 906, charge) relates the town's relationship with the sea, with model boats, treasure from local wrecks and stuffed fish.

Casa das Histórias

MAP P.119

Avda da República 300

ⓦ casadashistoriaspaularego.com, charge.

The distinctive ochre towers of the modernist **Casa das Histórias** mark a fantastic museum which,

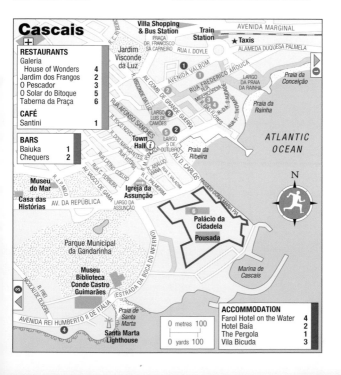

Cascais

RESTAURANTS
Galeria	
House of Wonders	4
Jardim dos Frangos	2
O Pescador	3
O Solar do Bitoque	5
Taberna da Praça	6

CAFÉ
| Santini | 1 |

BARS
| Baiuka | 1 |
| Chequers | 2 |

Villa Shopping & Bus Station
Train Station
★ Taxis
AVENIDA MARGINAL
PRAÇA DR. FRANCISCO SÁ CARNEIRO
ALAMEDA DUQUESA PALMELA
RUA I. DOYLE
Jardim Visconde da Luz
AVENIDA VALBOM
AV. COMB. DE GRANDE GUERRA
RUA VISCONDE DA LUZ
RUA FREDERICO AROUCA
LARGO DA PRAIA DA RAINHA
R. FDA. MISERICORDIA
R. DAS FLORES
R. SIMOEI
Praia da Conceição
Praia da Rainha
RUA AFONSO SANCHES
R. POÇO NOVO
LARGO LUIS DE CAMÕES
Town Hall ⓘ
LARGO 5 DE OUTUBRO
AV. D. CARLOS I
Praia da Ribeira
R. DAS NAVEGANTES
RUA DA VITORIA
RUA LATINO COELHO
R. DR. ABALIO
R. VIANA
R. L. PALMEIRA
R. VACALIM
PASSEIO D. MARIA PIA
ATLANTIC OCEAN
N
AV. VASCO DA GAMA
R. J. P. MELO
Museu do Mar
Casa das Histórias
AV. DA REPÚBLICA
R. C. FERREIRA
Igreja da Assunção
LARGO DA ASSUNÇÃO
Palácio da Cidadela
Pousada
Parque Municipal da Gandarinha
ESTRADA DA BOCA DO INFERNO
Museu Biblioteca Conde Castro Guimarães
Marina de Cascais
AVENIDA REI HUMBERTO II DE ITÁLIA
RUA NICOLAU DE OLIVEIRA
Praia de Santa Marta
Santa Marta Lighthouse
0 metres 100
0 yards 100

ACCOMMODATION
Farol Hotel on the Water	4
Hotel Baía	2
The Pergola	1
Vila Bicuda	3

unusually, is dedicated to Dame Paula Rego, who spent much of her life in the UK before she died in 2022. Designed by famous architect Eduardo Souto de Moura, the airy museum features over 120 of her disturbing but beautiful collages, pastels and engravings, as well as those by her late English husband Victor Willing. Many of her works explore themes of power: women and animals are portrayed as both powerful and sexually vulnerable; men often appear as fish or dressed in women's clothes.

Around Cascais Marina

MAP P.119

The leafy **Parque Municipal da Gandarinha**, complete with picnic tables and playground, makes a welcome escape from the beach crowds. In one corner stands the mansion of the nineteenth-century Count of Guimarães, preserved complete with its fittings

as the **Museu Biblioteca Conde Castro Guimarães** (Ⓦbit.ly/MuseuGuimaraes, charge). Its most valuable exhibits are rare illuminated sixteenth-century manuscripts.

Palácio da Cidadela

MAP P.119

Avda Dom Carlos I Ⓦ museu.presidencia.pt, charge.

To the east, the walls of Cascais' largely seventeenth-century **Citadela** (fortress) guard the entrance to the **Marina de Cascais**, an enclave of expensive yachts serviced by restaurants, bars and boutiques.

Originally a sea fort and then a summer retreat for Portuguese royalty, the Citadela has been used by the Portuguese president to entertain his guests ever since the declaration of the Republic in 1910. Today, you can wander around the lower-floor exhibition

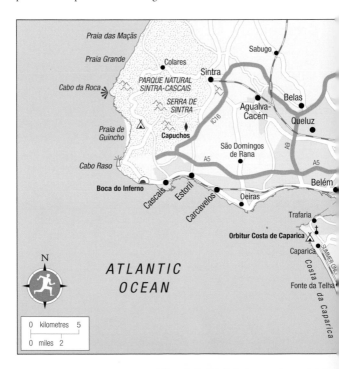

space, though it's worth the entrance fee to visit the top two floors (ask for a non-guided visit unless you understand Portuguese). There's also a lovely tearoom facing the ocean.

Caparica

MAP P.120
Via Rapida express 135 (roughly hourly; 30min) or slower local buses (every 15–30min; 50min), from Cacilhas or bus #161 from Lisbon's Praça Areeiro (every 30–60min; 40–60min).

According to legend, **Caparica** was named after the discovery of a cloak (*capa*) full of golden coins. Today it is a slightly tacky, high-rise seaside resort, but don't let that put you off: it's family-friendly, has plenty of good seafood as well as several kilometres of soft, sandy beach.

From the beach, a **narrow-gauge mini-railway** (June–Sept, charge) runs south along the beach for 8km to the resort of **Fonte da Telha**.

Surfers on the Costa da Caparica coastline

Jump off at any stop en route; earlier stops tend to be family-oriented, while nudity is common in later ones.

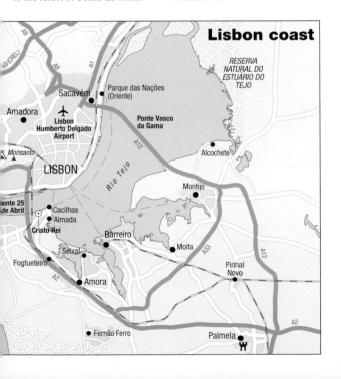

Restaurants

Baiuka

Praia das Moitas, Monte Estoril
Ⓦ **baiukabar.com.**
On the seafront promenade, about
10 minutes' walk from Cascais
towards Estoril, *Baiuka* has a sunny
terrace and makes a great and
quiet spot for a good value meal
or drink. Dishes include *carapau*
(mackerel), tuna steaks and salads
or inexpensive toasties. €€

Deck Bar

Arcadas do Parque 21–22, Estoril
Ⓦ **deckbar.pt.**
Facing Estoril's park, this great
little café-restaurant and bar has
appealing outdoor tables. It's a
good spot for a drink or snack,
and also serves a range of full
meals (salads, tortilla, fresh fish).
€€

The promenade in Cascais

Galeria House of Wonders

MAP P.119
Largo da Misericordia 53
Ⓦ **facebook.com/houseofwonders.**
This Dutch-run veggie café-
restaurant and gallery space has
an appealing, alternative vibe.
The street-level restaurant serves
amazing vegetarian meze of various
sizes: expect hummus, chickpea
salad and whatever fresh veg is in
season. There's a separate entrance
for the gallery space and laid-back
café, complete with a roof terrace
where you can relax for a drink on
old packing cases. €€

Jardim dos Frangos

MAP P.119
Avda Com. Grande Guerra 68, Cascais
Ⓣ **214 861 717.**
Permanently buzzing with people
and sizzling with the speciality,
bargain grilled chicken, which is
devoured by the plateful at indoor
and outdoor tables. Get there
early to secure a table as it is very
popular. €

O Barbas

Apoio de Praia 13, Caparica Ⓦ **obarbas.pt.**
Caparica's best-known beach
restaurant with affordable fish,
caldeirada (fish stew) and *arroz de
marisco* (seafood rice) to die for.
They also run the more upmarket
space next door, *O Barbas Tertúlia*,
though the menu is much the
same. €€

O Pescador

MAP P.119
Rua das Flores 10B, Cascais
Ⓦ **restaurantepescador.com.**
The best of a row of lively
restaurants near the centre, offering
upmarket seafood – expect superb
mains such as lobster baked in salt
or tuna cooked in olive oil and
garlic. €€€

O Solar do Bitoque

MAP P.119
**Rua Regimento 19 de Infantaria Loja 11,
Cascais** Ⓣ **214 061 102.**

Traditional *caldeirada*

Bitoques are thin steaks, and this lively local with outdoor seating specializes in various types, as well as burgers, salads and fresh fish. Very good value considering its position. €

Praia do Tamariz

Praia do Tamariz, Estoril ⓣ 214 681 010.
High-profile restaurant right on the promenade – which serves up good-value fish, meat, and sushi. Also a great spot for a sangria or *caipirinha* with lovely seaside views €€

Taberna da Praça

MAP P.119
Cidadela de Cascais, Avda Dom Carlos I ⓣ 214 814 300.
Tucked into a couple of cosy arched rooms within Cascais's impressive fortress, *Taberna da Praça* serves a range of tasty *petiscos*, the Portuguese version of tapas. You can sample regional specialities like scrambled eggs with smoked chicken chorizo, or grilled octopus with baked potatoes. There are also more substantial mains: great tuna steaks or duck rice. €€

Café

Santini

MAP P.119
Avda Valbom 28f ⓣ 214 833 709.
Opened by an Italian immigrant just after World War II, *Santini*'s delicious ice creams are legendary in these parts. €

Bars and clubs

Chequers

MAP P.119
Largo Luís de Camões 7, Cascais ⓣ 214 830 926.
An English-style pub that fills up early with a good-time crowd; it serves so-so meals, with weekend DJs and live football on TV, though most people come for drinks at tables outside in the attractive square.

Dr Bernard

Praia do CDS, Apoio de Praia 11, Caparica ⓦ drbernard.pt.
Jazzy seafront café-bar and also a surf school, and it's a great spot to nurse a drink or two while watching the local surfers show off their skills.

ACCOMMODATION

Hotel Avenida Palace

Accommodation

Lisbon's hotels range from sumptuous five-stars to backstreet hideaways packed with local character. The grander ones tend to be found along Avenida da Liberdade, around Parque Eduardo VII or out of the centre, though in recent years around forty have opened in the central Baixa where there are now endless options. Besides its hotels, Lisbon still has a few old-style guesthouses (*alojamento local* or *particular*, some of which keep the now abandoned titles of *pensão* or *residencial*) and various good-value hostels. Over the past decade or so, a wave of boutique-style hotels and guesthouses have sprung up across the city, often in old townhouses that have been transformed into stylish accommodation – these are usually reasonably priced and make for an atmospheric and comfortable stay. The Alfama and Bairro Alto, too, are beginning to offer a greater choice, with crumbling buildings being done up into hotels or smart self-catering apartments – often with great city or river views thanks to the districts' hilltop positions. Given the surge in new accommodation, it's rarely hard to find a decent room, except in high season. Prices given are for a night in the cheapest double room in high season. Rates drop considerably out of season. Unless otherwise stated, all the places reviewed below have an en-suite bath or shower and include breakfast (anything from bread, jam and coffee to a generous spread of rolls, cereals, croissants, cold meat, cheese and fruit).

The Baixa and Rossio

ALMALUSA MAP P.26, POCKET MAP D13. Praça do Município 21, tram #28 to Praça do Município Ⓦ almalusahotels.com. Beautifully positioned in the corner of a historic square, this eighteenth-century building now houses a chic boutique hotel. All the rooms are different, but each includes a smart TV and digital radio, and most have period touches such as flagstone floors and fireplaces. Front rooms overlook the town hall and tram routes. There's also a downstairs restaurant and small outdoor terrace. €€€

Accommodation Price Codes

€ - under 100 euros
€€ -100-150 euros
€€€ -150-200 euros
€€€€ - over 200 euros

Booking a room

The main tourist offices (see page 141) can provide accommodation lists, but won't reserve rooms for you. In the summer months, confirm a reservation at least a week in advance and get written confirmation; most owners understand English. Look out, too, for deals on hotel websites which are usually cheaper than walk-in rates.

HOTEL AVENIDA PALACE MAP P.26, POCKET MAP C11. **Rua 1 de Dezembro 123** Ⓜ **Restauradores** Ⓦ **hotelavenidapalace. pt.** Built at the end of the nineteenth century, and rumoured to have a secret door direct to neighbouring Rossio station, this is one of Lisbon's grandest hotels. Despite extensive modernization, the traditional feel has been maintained with chandeliers and period furniture throughout. There are 82 spacious rooms, each with high ceilings and colossal bathrooms. **€€€**

HOTEL MÉTROPOLE MAP P.26, POCKET MAP D11. **Rossio 30** Ⓜ **Restauradores** Ⓦ **almeidahotels.pt.** A welcoming three-star dating the early twentieth century, with an airy lounge-bar offering superb views over Rossio and the castle. The simply furnished but spacious rooms are comfortable, though the square can be quite noisy at night. **€€**

HOTEL PORTUENSE MAP P.26, POCKET MAP J5. **Rua das Portas de Santo Antão 149–157** Ⓜ **Restauradores** Ⓦ **hotelportuense.com.** Singles, doubles and triples in a family-run hotel in a great position. Decently decorated, all rooms come with a/c and TV. **€€**

LX ROSSIO MAP P.26, POCKET MAP D12. **Rua da Assunção 52** Ⓜ **Rossio** Ⓦ **lxrossiohotel.com.** One of the Baixa's most central options. With its own bar, the hotel's simple but comfortable rooms overlook relatively quiet pedestrianized streets. Triple rooms available. **€€**

RESIDENCIAL FLORESCENTE MAP P.26, POCKET MAP J5. **Rua das Portas de Santo Antão 99** Ⓜ **Restauradores** Ⓦ **residencialflorescente.com.** The best guesthouse on this pedestrianized street, with the bonus of having a small outdoor swimming pool. There's a large selection of air-conditioned rooms across four floors (some en suite with TV), so if you don't like the look of the room you're shown – and some are very cramped – ask about alternatives. Street-facing rooms can be noisy. There's also a lounge plus parking. **€€**

VIP EXECUTIVE ÉDEN MAP P.26, POCKET MAP C10. **Praça dos Restauradores 24** Ⓜ **Restauradores** Ⓦ **vipedenaparthotel.com.** Compact studios and apartments sleeping up to four people are available within the impressively converted Éden cinema. Get a ninth-floor apartment with a balcony and you'll have the best views and be just below the superb breakfast bar and rooftop pool. All come with dishwashers, microwaves and satellite TV, breakfast is extra. Disabled access. **Studios, from €€**

Self-catering

There are several fine options for self-catering in Lisbon. As well as Ⓦ airbnb.co.uk, good first points of call are Ⓦ fadoflats.pt (mostly in Chiado and Alfama) and Ⓦ castleinnlisbon.com, which has apartments right by the castle. Geared up to families is the upmarket Martinhal Chiado (Ⓦ martinhal.com) in the Chiado district (see page 129).

The Sé, Castelo and Alfama

1908 LISBOA HOTEL MAP P.38, POCKET MAP K5. **Largo do Intendente Pina Manique 6,** Ⓜ **Intendente** Ⓦ **1908lisboahotel.com** This superb Art Nouveau hotel is the top address in fashionable Largo do Intendente. Rooms at the southern end of the wedge-shaped building are smaller, but all are characterful and stylish, the nicest overlooking the pedestrianized square. A generous breakfast is served in the classy *Infame* restaurant downstairs (see page 47). €€€

ALBERGARIA SENHORA DO MONTE MAP P.38, POCKET MAP L5. **Calçada do Monte 39, Tram #28** Ⓦ **bit.ly/AlbergariaHotel.** Comfortable if slightly dated hotel in a sublime location with views of the castle and Graça convent from the south-facing rooms (avoid the north-facing ones), some of which have terraces. Breakfast is taken on the fourth-floor terrace. Free wi-fi and private parking are available. €€

MEMMO ALFAMA MAP P.38, POCKET MAP F12. **Trav Merceeiras 27, Tram #28** Ⓦ **memmoalfama.com.** Hidden behind the facade of a former house, paint factory and bakery lies this sleek boutique hotel. Parts of the ground floor contain the old brick ovens, though the real appeal is the bar with terraces at the back, complete with small plunge pool, offering sumptuous views over the Alfama and the Tagus. Rooms are compact, but have all mod cons and most boast fine views. €€€

PALACETE CHAFARIZ D'EL REI MAP P.38, POCKET MAP G12. **Trav Chafariz d'El Rei 6, Tram #25** Ⓦ **chafarizdelrei.com.** Luxury guesthouse built in 1909 by a wealthy Brazilian merchant and lovingly restored a century later. From the reception – flooded with light from stained-glass windows – to the mirror room and library, the house is a stunning mix of Brazilian Art Nouveau and neo-Arabic flamboyance. Huge rooms, most with river views, have chandeliers and modern bathrooms, while stonking breakfasts keep you going till dinner time. It also has its own "tea house", serving tasty Portuguese dishes in an ornate dining room. €€€€

SOLAR DO CASTELO MAP P.38, POCKET MAP F11. **Rua das Cozinhas 2, Bus #37** Ⓦ **lisbonheritagehotels.com.** A tastefully renovated eighteenth-century mansion abutting the castle walls on the site of the former palace kitchens, parts of which remain. Its 14 rooms cluster around a tranquil inner courtyard, where you can enjoy a vast buffet breakfast. Rooms aren't enormous, but most boast balconies overlooking the castle grounds, and service is second to none. €€€

SOLAR DOS MOUROS MAP P.38, POCKET MAP F12. **Rua do Milagre de Santo António 6, Tram #28** Ⓦ **solardosmouroslisboa. com.** A tall Alfama townhouse done out in a contemporary style with its own bar. Each of the twelve rooms offers fantastic vistas of the river or castle. There's plenty of modern art to enjoy if you tire of the view. €€€

Chiado and Cais do Sodré

HOTEL BAIRRO ALTO MAP P.52, POCKET MAP C12. **Praça Luís de Camões 2** Ⓜ **Baixa-Chiado** Ⓦ **bairroaltohotel.com.** In the middle of trendy Chiado, this grand eighteenth-century building has been modernized into a fashionable boutique hotel. Rooms and communal areas still have a period feel, but a fantastic contemporary extension by architect Eduardo Souto de Moura brings the building bang into the twenty-first century. The rooms have all the luxuries you'd expect, with great views from the top floor ones – and from the trendy rooftop café-bar. €€€€

HOTEL BORGES MAP P.52, POCKET MAP C12. **Rua Garrett 108 Ⓜ Baixa-Chiado** Ⓦ hotelborges.com. In a prime spot on Chiado's main street, this traditional and elegantly furnished three-star is very popular, though front rooms can be noisy. Double or triple rooms come in a variety of styles, but all are good value. €€

HOTEL DO CHIADO MAP P.52, POCKET MAP D12. **Rua Nova do Almada 114 Ⓜ Baixa-Chiado** Ⓦ hoteldochiado.pt. Designed by architect Álvaro Siza Vieira, this stylish hotel has lovely communal areas – orange segment-shaped windows give glimpses of Chiado in one direction and the whole city in the other. The cheapest rooms lack much of an outlook, but the best ones have terraces with stunning views towards the castle – a view you get from the bar terrace too. Limited parking available. €€€

LX BOUTIQUE MAP P.52, POCKET MAP C13. **Rua do Alecrim 12 Ⓜ Cais do Sodré** Ⓦ lxboutiquehotel.com. A tasteful makeover to an old townhouse has transformed *LX Boutique* into a popular small hotel with its own chic restaurant. The "boutique" refers to its themed floors, named after Portuguese poets and fado singers. Rooms are all stylish and individual, with shutters and tasteful lighting – try and get one with river views rather than over the late-night Rua Nova do Carvalho. €€€

MARTINHAL CHIADO MAP P.52, POCKET MAP C13. **Rua Flores 44 Ⓜ Baixa-Chiado** Ⓦ martinhal.com. Taking up an entire block on the steep Rua Flores, this welcoming hotel is geared up to making family holidays a luxurious treat. Bright, spacious apartments come with their own kitchenettes if you want to self-cater, and most come with comfy bunks for kids either alongside or in a separate room from large double beds. There's a kids' club, crèche, vaulted play room and an alluring real car to clamber into in the breakfast room. The studios would also make an ideal base for couples too. **Studios/apartments** €€€€

Bairro Alto and São Bento

CASA DE SÃO MAMEDE MAP P.60, POCKET MAP H5. **Rua da Escola Politécnica 159, Bus #1** Ⓦ casadesaomamede.pt. On a busy street north of Príncipe Real, this is a superb eighteenth-century former magistrate's house with period fittings, bright breakfast room and a grand stained-glass window. Rooms are rather ordinary, but all are equipped with a TV and a/c. €

HOTEL BELVER PRINCÍPE REAL MAP P.60, POCKET MAP H5. **Rua da Alegria 53, Bus #1** Ⓦ belverhotels.com. This small four-star sits on a quiet street just below the Bairro Alto. Eighteen rooms come with modern decor, some with balconies and superb city views. Best of all is the top-floor suite with stunning vistas. €€

THE INDEPENDENTE HOSTEL & SUITES MAP P.60, POCKET MAP B10. **Rua de São Pedro de Alcântara 81** Ⓦ theindependente. pt. This part-hostel, part-boutique hotel is set in a fantastic old building with far-reaching views over Lisbon. Lower floors house dorms (sleeping 6–12) with towering ceilings. Upstairs are quirky double rooms in the roof spaces, the best with balconies offering river views. There's a downstairs bar and patio, and the place offers everything from bar crawls to guided walks and cycle hire. The Suites element is in the building next door, offering larger rooms, a library and a hip bar on the roof terrace. **Dorms €, Doubles/suites** €€

PENSÃO LONDRES MAP P.60, POCKET MAP B10. **Rua Dom Pedro V 53, Bus #1** Ⓦ pensaolondres.com.pt. Wonderful old building with high ceilings and pleasant enough rooms sleeping up to four. Some have tiny bathrooms, but the best (ask for rooms 402, 409 or 411) have great views over the city. €

Estrela, Lapa and Santos

AS JANELAS VERDES MAP P.73, POCKET MAP G8. **Rua das Janelas Verdes 47, Bus #727 or tram #25** Ⓦ asjanelasverdes. com. This discreet eighteenth-century townhouse, where Eça de Queirós was inspired to write *Os Maias*, is just metres from the Museu de Arte Antiga. The spacious rooms come with marble bathrooms and period furnishings, most with views of the Tejo. Breakfast is served in the delightful walled garden in summer, while the top-floor library and terrace command spectacular river views. €€€€

OLISSIPPO LAPA PALACE MAP P.73, POCKET MAP F7. **Rua do Pau da Bandeira 4** W lapapalace.com. A stunning nineteenth-century mansion set in its own lush gardens, with dramatic vistas over the Tejo. Rooms are luxurious, and those in the Palace Wing are each decorated in a different style, from Classical to Art Deco. There's also a health club, disabled access and a list of facilities as long as your arm, from babysitting to banqueting. €€€€

YORK HOUSE MAP P.73, POCKET MAP G7. **Rua das Janelas Verdes 32, Bus #727 or tram #25** W yorkhouselisboa.com. Located in a sixteenth-century Carmelite convent (and hidden from the main street by high walls), rooms here are chic and minimalist. The best are grouped around a beautiful interior courtyard, where drinks and meals are served in summer, and there's a highly rated restaurant. Advance bookings recommended. €€€

Alcântara and Belém

JERÓNIMOS 8 MAP P.84, POCKET MAP C4. **Rua das Jerónimos 8, Tram #15** W almediahotels.pt. In a great position for Belém's attractions, this hotel is housed in an attractive stone building with boutique touches – crisp white decor, marble bathrooms and a modern bar area, plus a substantial buffet breakfast. €€€€

PESTANA PALACE MAP P.78, POCKET MAP C8. **Rua Jau 54, Tram #18** W pestanapalacelisbon.com. Set in an early twentieth-century palace full of priceless works of art, most beds at this five-star hotel are in tasteful modern wings that stretch either side of lush gardens. Most rooms have large terraces and lie a short walk from a cocktail bar, a sunken outdoor pool with a fountain to swim out to, and an indoor pool and health club. The price, which can be greatly reduced for

summer offers, includes a vast breakfast in the former ballroom. €€€€

Avenida, Parque Eduardo VII and the Gulbenkian

CASA AMORA MAP P.92, POCKET MAP G5. **Alto de São Francisco 25** M **Rato** W casaamora.com. Close to the picturesque Praça das Amoreiras, there are six tastefully furnished studios with their own kitchenettes which are suitable for families. There's also an attractive outdoor patio. €€

DOUBLE TREE FONTANA PARK MAP P.92, POCKET MAP J3. **Rua Eng. Viera da Silva 2** M **Saldanha** W bit.ly/ DoubleTreeFontanaPark. This buzzy designer hotel rises sleekly behind the facade of an old steelworks. Chic rooms – the best with terraces – come with Philippe Starck chromatic baths. The communal areas include a restaurant, bar and a courtyard garden with slate walls of running water. Cocktail nights with guest DJs complete the picture. €€€

EUROSTAR DAS LETRAS MAP P.92, POCKET MAP H5. **Rua Castilho 6–12** M **Avenida** W eurostarshotels.com. Modern hotel with its own small gym and bar in a good position between the centre and the Bairro Alto. Rooms, named after writers, come with comfy beds, a choice of pillows and a complicated array of power showers. The best have balconies with downtown views. €€€

HERITAGE AVENIDA LIBERDADE MAP P.92, POCKET MAP J5. **Avda da Liberdade 28** M **Restauradores** W heritageavliberdade.com. In a fine mansion – whose ground floor once sold herbal remedies (the counter still remains) – this hotel superbly blends tradition and contemporary style. Though the dining area/ bar is small (and the gym/plunge pool even smaller), the rooms more than compensate with retro fittings and great cityscapes from top-floor rooms. €€€

HOTEL AVENIDA PARK MAP P.92, POCKET MAP H4. **Avda Sidónio Pais 6** M **Parque** W avenidapark.com. Good-sized rooms – beg for one with a view over the park for no extra charge – in a friendly, if dated, hotel on a quiet street. €€

HOTEL BRITANIA MAP P.92, POCKET MAP J5. Rua Rodrigues Sampaio 17 Ⓜ Avenida Ⓦ hotel-britania.com. Designed in the 1940s by influential architect Cassiano Branco, this Art Deco gem features huge airy rooms, each with traditional cork flooring and marble-clad bathrooms. The hotel interior, with library and bar, has been declared of national architectural importance. €€€

HOTEL DOM CARLOS PARQUE MAP P.92, POCKET MAP H4. Avda Duque de Loulé 121 Ⓜ Marquês de Pombal Ⓦ hoteldomcarlospark.com. Decent three-star just off Praça Marquês de Pombal, with fair-sized rooms over eight floors, each with plasma TV. Some overlook the neighbouring police and fire stations, which can add to the noise. There's a downstairs lounge bar and garage parking. €€

INSPIRA LIBERDADE BOUTIQUE MAP P.92, POCKET MAP J4. Rua de Santa Marta 48 Ⓦ inspirahotels.com. The facade of a traditional townhouse hides a modern boutique hotel which boasts impressive green credentials, including low-energy lighting and recycled or local products. Feng shui-designed rooms are compact but comfy with glass-wall showers, coffee-making facilities and free minibars. There's also a spa, games room, stylish restaurant and bar. €€€

LISBOA PLAZA MAP P.92, POCKET MAP J5. Trav Salitre 7 Ⓜ Avenida Ⓦ lisbonplazahotel.com. A tasteful, understated former Portuguese family home with marble bathrooms, a bar and fashionable rooftop terrace, a short walk from the main Avenida. Friendly staff and good for families. Limited disabled access. €€€

NH COLLECTION LISBOA LIBERDADE MAP P.92, POCKET MAP J5. Avda da Liberdade 180b Ⓜ Avenida Ⓦ nh-hotels.com. Discreetly tucked into the back of the Tivoli forum shopping centre off the main Avenida, this Spanish chain hotel offers

ten floors of modern flair. The best rooms have balconies facing the traditional Lisbon houses at the back. Unusually for central Lisbon, there's a rooftop pool. There's also a bar and restaurant. €€€

SANA REX MAP P.92, POCKET MAP G4. Rua Castilho 169 Ⓜ Marquês de Pombal/Parque Ⓦ rex.sanahotels.com. One of the less outrageously priced hotels in this neck of the woods, with small but well-equipped rooms and a bar. The best rooms are at the front, sporting large balconies overlooking Parque Eduardo VII. €

SHERATON LISBOA MAP P.92, POCKET MAP J3. Rua Latino Coelho 1 Ⓜ Picoas Ⓦ bit.ly/SheratonLisboa. This 1970s high-rise is something of an icon in this part of Lisbon and a mecca for those seeking five-star spa facilities. The dated exterior hides modern attractions, including a heated outdoor pool, swanky rooms and a top-floor bar and restaurant with dazzling city views. €€€€

Sintra

CASA DO VALLE MAP P.110. Rua da Paderna 2 Ⓦ casadovalle.com. Though steeply downhill from the historic centre, this charming guesthouse still commands unbeatable views across the wooded slopes of Sintra. There are various rooms, from top-floor doubles with the best views, to ground-floor rooms with their own terraces. All rooms access a beautiful garden with its own pool. Good for families. Breakfast is extra. €

CHALET RELOGIO MAP P.110. Estrada da Pena 22, Sintra-Vila ☎ 963 966 325. Architect Luigi Manini, who worked on the Quinta da Regaleira (see page 111), designed this mansion with a distinctive clock tower. Rooms are simply furnished but enormous, with big windows and high ceilings, and there's a garden too, though it's a long walk to town and you'll need a car. €

CHALET SAUDADE MAP P.110. Rua Dr. Alfredo Costa 21 Ⓦ saudade.pt. This tall eighteenth-century chalet has been superbly renovated by a Portuguese couple who have retained many of the quirky but charming original fittings. The interior is all parquet flooring, swirling stairways, stained glass and beautiful *azulejos*. Stairs take you down three floors to rooms of varying sizes: if possible, pay extra to bag the one opening onto the garden. Breakfast is offered at *Saudade Café* (see page 117). €

HOTEL ARRIBAS MAP P.113. Avda A Coelho 28, Praia Grande ⓦ hotelarribas. pt. This three-star is plonked ungraciously above the beach. Large rooms come with minibars and satellite TV – those with a sea view are hard to fault – while family rooms sleep up to four. There's also a massive sea-water swimming pool, a restaurant and café terrace, and disabled access. €€€

HOTEL NOVA SINTRA MAP P.110. Largo Afonso de Albuquerque 25, Estefânia ⓦ novasintra.com. A friendly hotel in a big mansion, whose elevated terrace-café overlooks a busy street. The modern rooms all have cable TV and shiny marble floors, and there's a decent restaurant. Two-night minimum stay in high season. €€

HOTEL SINTRA JARDIM MAP P.110. Trav dos Avelares 12, São Pedro ⓦ hotelsintrajardim.pt. The best mid-range option in the area, this rambling old hotel has soaring ceilings, wooden floors and oodles of character. In winter there's a log fire in the communal lounge. There's a substantial garden with a swimming pool, and the giant rooms can easily accommodate extra beds, so it's great for families. Book ahead in summer. €€

SÃO SATURNINO MAP P.113. Azóia ⓦ saosat.com. Reached down a steep track – look for the sign left just past the turning to Cabo da Roca, before Azóia – this former convent dates back to the twelfth century and sits in a valley where time seems to stand still. The six rooms, three suites and self-catering apartment are traditionally furnished, while the rambling communal areas are all weathered beams, bare bricks and low ceilings. There's a small outdoor pool, barbecue area, geese, cats

and terraces with stunning views – truly magical. €€

Lisbon coast

FAROL HOTEL ON THE WATER MAP P.119. Avda Rei Humberto II de Italia 7, Cascais ⓦ farol.com.pt. Right on the seafront, this is one of the area's most fashionable hideaways, neatly combining traditional and contemporary architecture. A new designer wing has been welded onto a sixteenth-century villa, and the decor combines wood and marble with modern steel and glass. The best rooms have sea views and terraces. There's also a restaurant, fairy-lit outside bar and seapool facing a fine rocky foreshore. €€€€

HOTEL BAÍA MAP P.119. Avda Marginal, Cascais ⓦ hotelbaia.com. Large seafront hotel boasting 113 rooms with a/c and satellite TV; front ones have balconies overlooking the beach. There's a great rooftop terrace complete with a covered pool, and a good restaurant. Parking is extra. €€

THE PERGOLA MAP P.119. Avda Valbom 13, Cascais ⓦ thepergola.pt. Sumptuous century-old mansion in the centre of town, with its own garden, stucco ceilings and wonderfully ornate tiled dining room. Each room has its own distinct character, some with their own balconies. €€

REAL CAPARICA HOTEL Rua Mestre Manuel 18, Caparica ⓦ bit.ly/RealCaparica. Friendly and reasonably-priced central hotel, a few minutes' walk from the beach, just off Rua dos Pescadores. Small but pleasant rooms come with TVs and baths. Ask for one of the rooms with a balcony and sea views. €

VILA BICUDA MAP P.119. Rua dos Faisões, Cascais ⓦ vilabicuda.com. A very well-run, upmarket villa complex set in its own grounds, with two large swimming pools. Excellent for families, the modern villas are well equipped and the complex has its own great café, shop and (pricey) Italian restaurant. But you'll need a car – it's around 3km from central Cascais towards Guincho. Studios €€

Lisbon hostels

Lisbon and its surroundings have some of Europe's best independent hostels. A youth hostel card is required for the official Portuguese hostels (*pousadas de juventude*), but you can buy one on your first night's stay. Unless stated, prices do not include breakfast.

Hostels

HOME HOSTEL MAP P.26, POCKET MAP E12. **Rua de São Nicolau 13-2** Ⓦ homelisbonhostel.com. In the heart of the Baixa, this highly rated hostel comes with four, six or eight-bed dorms, double rooms, fantastic home-cooking, a buzzy communal lounge and the opportunity to sign up to walking tours and pub nights. **Dorms €, doubles €€€**

LISBON LOUNGE HOSTEL MAP P.26, POCKET MAP D12. **Rua de São Nicolau 41** Ⓜ Rossio Ⓦ lisbonlounge.com. A popular independent hostel in a great old Baixa townhouse full of stripped floorboards, comfy sofas and books. Breakfast and dinner on request. **Dorms/twins €**

LOST INN MAP P.52, POCKET MAP C13. **Beco dos Apóstolos 6** Ⓜ Baixa-Chiado Ⓦ lostinnlisbon.com. In a great old building on a quiet side street a short walk from Chiado or Cais do Sodré, this hostel has six- to ten-bed mixed or single-sex dorms and cosy doubles. There's also a bar, dining area and communal kitchen. **Dorms/twins €**

MOON HILL HOSTEL MAP P.110. **Rua Guilherme Gomes Fernandes 17, Sintra** Ⓦ moonhillhostel.com. This fantastic hostel has friendly staff, stylish decor and a range of contemporary rooms, from en-suite doubles to dorms with bunk beds. There's a communal kitchen and lounge with a wood burner for the winter, and a terrace and patio to unwind in the summer. **Dorms/doubles €**

POUSADA DE JUVENTUDE DE OEIRAS Estrada Marginal, Oeiras Ⓦ pousadasjuventude.pt. This hostel is set in an eighteenth-century sea-fort overlooking the sea pools in Oeiras, a suburb on the train line to Cascais. Parking is available. **Dorms/twins €**

POUSADA DE JUVENTUDE DE LISBOA MAP P.92, POCKET MAP H3. **Rua Andrade Corvo 46** Ⓜ Picoas Ⓦ pousadasjuventude. pt. The main city hostel, set in a rambling old building, with a small bar, canteen, TV room and disabled access. There are 30 dorms sleeping four to six, as well as en-suite rooms. Price includes breakfast. **Dorms/doubles €**

POUSADA DE JUVENTUDE LISBOA PARQUE DAS NAÇÕES MAP P.104, POCKET MAP A16. **Rua de Moscavide 47–101, Parque das Nações** Ⓜ Oriente Ⓦ pousadasjuventude.pt. About a five-minute walk northeast of the Torre Vasco da Gama, towards the bridge, this smart, modern youth hostel has a pool table and disabled access. **Dorms/doubles €**

ESSENTIALS

Make time for a coffee and a *pastéis de nata*

Arrival

Lisbon airport is right on the edge of the city and is well served by buses and taxis. The city's train stations are all centrally located and connected to the metro; the main bus station is also close to metro and train stops.

By plane

Humberto Delgado Airport, or Lisbon Airport, (☎ 218 413 500, ⓦ aeroportolisboa.pt) is north of the city centre and has a tourist office (☎ 218 450 660; daily 7am–midnight), a 24hr exchange bureau and left-luggage facilities.

The easiest way into the city is by **taxi**; a journey to Rossio should cost around €15. The airport is also on the red Oriente line of the **metro** (see page 136), although you'll need to change at Alameda for the centre. **Local bus** #744 also runs to Praça Marquês de Pombal (every 10–15min; €2), but is less convenient if you have a lot of luggage.

By train

Long-distance **trains** are run by CP (Comboios de Portugal, ⓦ cp.pt). You'll arrive at Santa Apolónia station, from where you can access the Gaivota metro line or take a bus west to Praça do Comércio. Some trains stop at Entrecampos (on the Amarela line) or at Oriente station (on the Oriente line) at Parque das Nações. These stations are more convenient for the airport or northern Lisbon.

By bus

The national **bus** carrier is Rede Expressos (ⓦ rede-expressos.pt). Most services terminate at Sete Rios, next to the Jardim Zoológico metro stop (for the centre) and Sete Rios train line (for Sintra and the northern suburbs). Some bus services also stop at the Oriente station at Parque das Nações on the Oriente metro line.

By car

Apart from weekends, when the city is quiet, **driving** round Lisbon is best avoided, though it is useful to hire a car to see the outlying sights. Parking is difficult in central Lisbon. Pay-and-display spots get snapped up quickly and the unemployed get by on tips for guiding drivers into empty spots. It may be easier heading for an official car park, for which you pay around €2–3 an hour or €15 a day. Do not leave valuables inside your car.

Getting around

Central Lisbon is compact enough to explore on **foot**, but don't be fooled by the apparent closeness of sights as they appear on maps. There are some very steep hills to negotiate, although the city's quirky *elevadores* (funicular railways) will save you the steepest climbs. Tram, bus and *elevador* stops are indicated by a sign marked "paragem", which carries route details.

Metro stations (ⓜ) are located close to most of the main sights. Suburban trains run from Rossio and Sete Rios stations to Sintra and from Cais do Sodré station to Belém, Estoril and Cascais, while ferries (ⓦ transtejo.pt) link Lisbon's Cais do Sodré to Cacilhas, for the resort of Caparica.

The metro

Lisbon's efficient **metro** (Metropolitano, daily 6.30am–1am, ⓦ metrolisboa.pt) is the quickest way of reaching the city's main sights, with trains every few minutes. Tickets cost €1.65 per journey, or €1.50 with a Viva Viagem card (see page 137) – sold at all stations (see the inside cover and pull-out map for the network diagram).

Buses and trams

City trams and buses (daily 6.30am–midnight) are operated by Carris (Ⓦcarris.pt). **Buses** (*autocarros*) run just about everywhere in the Lisbon area – the most useful ones are outlined in the box below.

Trams (*eléctricos*) run on six routes, which are marked on the chapter maps. Ascending some of the steepest urban gradients in the world, most are worth taking for the ride alone, especially the cross-city tram #28 (see page 43). Another picturesque route is #12, which circles the castle area via Largo Martim Moniz. Other useful routes are "supertram" #15 from Praça da Figueira to Belém (signed Algés), and #18, which runs from Cais do Sodré via Praça do Comércio to the Palácio da Ajuda. Tram #25, runs from near the Praça da Figueira to Campo Ourique via Santos, Lapa and Estrela. The remaining route, #24, runs from Praça Luís Camões in Chiado to Compolide, via the Bairro Alto.

Elevadores

There are also several **elevadores**. These consist of two funicular railways offering quick access to the heights of the Bairro Alto (see pages 58 and 59) and to the eastern side of Avenida da Liberdade (see page 90); and one giant lift, the Elevador da Santa Justa (see page 29) which goes up to the foot of the Bairro Alto near Chiado. There are also free street lifts offering access to the lower edges of the Castelo de São Jorge (see map page 38).

Tickets and passes

On board **tickets** cost €2 (buses), €3 (trams), €3.80 for *elevadores* (valid for two trips) and €5.30 for the Elevador da Santa Justa. You need to get a separate card for train lines to Sintra or Cascais. Note that the modern tram #15 has an automatic ticket machine on board and does not issue change.

It's possible just to buy a ticket each time you ride, but **passes**, available from any main metro station, can save you money. First, buy a rechargeable Viva Viagem card (€0.50), which you can load up with up to €3–40, after which €1.50 is deducted for each bus or metro journey.

You can also buy a one-day Bilhete 1dia pass (€6.65, or €10.70 including trains to Sintra and Cascais), which allows unlimited travel on buses, trams, the metro and *elevadores* for 24 hours after it is first used.

If you're planning some intensive sightseeing, the Cartão Lisboa (Ⓦwww.lisboarcard.org; €22 for one day, €37 for two days, €46 for three) is a good buy. The card entitles you to unlimited rides on buses, trams, *elevadores* and

---

Useful bus routes

#201 Night bus from Cais do Sodré to the docks via Santos; until 5am.

#728 Belém to Parque das Nações via Santa Apolónia station.

#737 Praça da Figueira to Castelo de São Jorge via the Sé and Alfama.

#744 Outside the airport to Marquês de Pombal via Saldanha and Picoas (for the youth hostel).

#727 Marquês de Pombal to Belém via Santos and Alcântara.

#773 Rato to Alcântara via Príncipe Real, Estrela and Lapa.

Sightseeing tours

Bus and tram tours Yellow Buses (ⓦ yellowbustours.com) offer tours around various parts of the city for €45, including the Hills Tram tour on a historic tram, a bus and tram tour which includes a bus to Belém and Parque das Naçoes and a boat, bus and tram tour taking in the above plus a ride on the river. Each tour lasts around 90 minutes, tickets are valid for at least 72 hours and include free use of Lisbon's other trams and funiculars.

River cruises Various boat tours take in the sights of Lisbon from the river, most leaving from the Sul Sueste ferry terminal (see map page 26) by Praça do Comércio. Expect to pay €20–30 for a 90-minute tour. A fun option is a 90-minute land and river tour offered by Hippotrip (ⓦ hippotrip.com; €30) on an amphibious vehicle, with departures from Doca de Santo Amaro.

Walks Recommended themed two- to three-hour guided walks are offered by Lisbon Walker (ⓦ lisbonwalker.com; €20), departing daily from Praça do Comércio at 10am, giving expert insight into the quirkier aspects of the city's sites, including secret histories and spies.

Segway and cycle tours Lisbon Segway Tours (ⓦ lisbonsegwaytours.pt) do various Segway tours of the city from around €45 for two hours; they also offer e-bike tours (€65 for three hours) or regular bike tours (€55 for two hours).

Tuk-tuk tours Various companies offer tours in three-wheeled tuk-tuks that can negotiate Lisbon's steepest and narrow streets around the Alfama. Prices start at around €45 an hour and depart from outside the Sé cathedral and also Sintra train station.

the metro as well as free entry to or discounts for around 25 museums. It's available online and from all the main tourist offices. The same website also has discount passes for Sintra.

Taxis

Lisbon's cream **taxis** have a minimum charge of €3.25; an average ride across town is €10–15. Fares are twenty percent higher from 9pm to 6am, at weekends and on public holidays. Bags in the boot incur a €1.60 fee. Meters should be switched on, and tips are not expected. Outside the rush hour taxis can be flagged down quite easily, or head for one of the ranks such as those outside the main train stations. At night, it's best to phone a taxi (attracts an extra charge of €0.80): try Teletaxis (☏ 218 111 100; ⓦ teletaxis. pt). Alternatively, Uber operate throughout the city (ⓦ uber.com).

Car rental

Rental agents include: Avis ⓦ avis. com.pt; Budget ⓦ budget.com.pt; Europcar ⓦ europcar.com; Hertz airport ⓦ hertz.com. For more information on driving in Lisbon see page 136.

Directory A–Z

Accessible Travel

Lisbon airport offers a service for **wheelchair-users** if advance notice is given to your airline (details on ⓦ aeroportolisboa.pt), while the Orange Badge symbol is recognized

Eating Out

Prices are based on a two-course meal for one with a drink.
€ - under 20 euros
€€ - 21-35 euros
€€€ - 36-50 euros
€€€€ - over 50 euros

for disabled car parking. The main public transport company, Carris, offers an inexpensive dial-a-ride minibus service, O Serviço Mobilidade Reduzida especial, (€2 per trip; Mon–Fri 6.30am–9.30pm, Sat & Sun 8am–noon & 2–6pm; ☎ 213 613 141, Ⓦ bit.ly/CarrisServices), though two days' advance notice and a medical certificate are required.

Addresses

Addresses are written in the form "Rua do Crucifixo 50–4°", meaning the fourth storey of no. 50, Rua do Crucifixo. The addition of e, d or r/c at the end means the entrance is on the left (*esquerda*), right (*direita*) or the ground floor (*rés-do-chão*).

Bike hire

Most of Lisbon is very hilly, but the riverfront is flat and good for bike hire. There are bike hire outlets at Belém (see page 83) and Doca de Santo Amaro (Armazém 7 ☎ 218 250 266; daily 10am–7pm). Expect to pay around €5 an hour.

Children

Portugal is very child-friendly, and kids are welcome in most restaurants and cafés. While dedicated children's menus are rare, most restaurants will serve a half-portion (*meia dose*) of dishes from the menu. Beware that many of the streets are narrow,

cobbled and steep, so can be awkward for pushchairs.

Cinemas

Mainstream **films** are shown at various multiplexes around the city, usually with Portuguese subtitles. Listings can be found on Ⓦ agendalx.pt. The Instituto da Cinemateca Portuguesa (Rua Barata Salgueiro 39 Ⓜ Avenida Ⓦ cinemateca.pt), the national film theatre, has twice-daily shows and contains its own cinema museum.

Crime

Violent crime is very rare, but pickpocketing is common, especially on public transport.

Electricity

Portugal uses two-pin plugs (220/240v). UK appliances will work with a continental adaptor.

Embassies and consulates

Australia, Avenida da Liberdade 2002 Ⓜ Avenida; ☎ 213 101 500; Canada, Avenida da Liberdade 198–200-3° Ⓜ Avenida; ☎ 213 164 600; Ireland, Avenida da Liberdade 200-4° Ⓜ Avenida; ☎ 213 308 200; South Africa, Avda Luís Bivar 10 Ⓜ Picoas; ☎ 213 192 200; UK, Rua de São Bernardo 33 Ⓜ Rato; ☎ 213 924 000, Ⓦ gov.uk/world/portugal; US, Avenida das Forças Armadas, Ⓜ Jardim Zoológico; ☎ 217 273 300, Ⓦ pt.usembassy.gov.

Emergencies

For police, fire and ambulance services, dial ☎ 112

Event listings

The best listings magazine is the free monthly *Agenda Cultural* (ⓦ agendalx. pt) produced by the town hall (in Portuguese). *Follow me Lisboa* is an English-language version produced by the local tourist office. Both are available from the tourist offices and larger hotels and can be downloaded from ⓦ visitlisboa.com.

Health

Pharmacies, the first point of call if you are ill, are open Mon–Fri 9am–1pm & 3–7pm, Sat 9am–1pm. Details of **24hr pharmacies** are posted on every pharmacy door, or call ☏ 118. The most central hospital is Hospital de Santa Maria (Avenida Prof. Egas Moniz ⓜ Entre Campos ☏ 217 805 000, ⓦ www.chln.pt), which is part of the North Lisbon University Hospital Center (CHULN). There are various other public hospitals around the city. EU residents are entitled to access public medical care, as long as they obtain a European Health Insurance Card (EHIC) before they travel. Following the UK's departure from the EU, once their EHIC cards expire, British nationals must apply for a Global Health Insurance Card (GHIC), available from ⓦ bit.ly/GHICCard. Despite the reciprocal arrangement afforded by this system, some form of additional private medical insurance is recommended.

Internet

Most hotels offer free wi-fi and often have computers for public use in reception. Most large cafés, bars and restaurants also offer free wi-fi.

Left luggage

There are 24hr lockers at the airport, main train and bus station, charging around €5 per day; for alternative venues around the city, check ⓦ radicalstorage.com.

LGBTQ+ travellers

The Centro Comunitário Gay e Lésbico de Lisboa (Rua dos Fanqueiros 40; ⓜ Martim Moniz; ☏ 218 873 918; Wed–Sat 7–11pm;) is the main gay and lesbian community centre, run by ILGA, whose website (ⓦ ilga-portugal.pt) is in Portuguese.

Lost property

Report any loss to the **tourist police** station in the Foz Cultura building in Palácio Foz, Praça dos Restauradores (daily 24hr ☏ 213 421 634). For items left on public transport, contact ⓦ carris.pt.

Money

Portugal uses the **euro** (€). Banks open Monday to Friday 8.30am–3pm. Most central branches have automatic exchange machines for various currencies. You can withdraw up to €300 per day from ATMs ("Multibanco") with a maximum €200 per transaction – check fees with your home bank. Credit/debit cards are widely accepted, as are contactless payments.

Opening hours

Most **shops** open Monday to Saturday 9am–7pm; smaller shops close for lunch (around 1–3pm) and on Saturday afternoons; shopping centres are open daily until 10pm or later. Most **museums** and **monuments** open Tuesday to Sunday from around 10am–6pm; details are given in the Guide.

Opera

Lisbon's main opera house is the Rococo Teatro Nacional São Carlos (Rua Serpa Pinto 9; ⓦ tnsc.pt).

Phones

Most European-subscribed **mobile phones** will work in Lisbon, and those with mobiles from EU countries will pay no additional roaming charges. For other nationalities, including British visitors post-Brexit, it's best to check with your provider whether there are extra charges for using roaming minutes and data while in Portugal before you travel.

Post

Post offices (*correios*) are usually open Monday to Friday 8.30am–6.30pm. The main Lisbon office at Praça dos Restauradores 58 is open until 9pm, Mon–Fri (☏ 210 471 616). Stamps (*selos*) are sold at post offices and anywhere that has the sign "Correio de Portugal – Selos" displayed.

Smoking

In common with most other EU countries, smoking is prohibited in most restaurants and cafés.

Sports

Lisbon boasts two of Europe's top **football** teams (see page 98): Benfica (ⓦ slbenfica.pt) and Sporting (ⓦ sporting.pt). Fixtures and news on ⓦ ligaportugal.pt. The area also contains some of Europe's best **golf courses**, especially around Cascais and Estoril (info at ⓦ portugalgolf. pt). The Atlantic beaches at Caparica and Guincho are ideal for **surfing** and windsurfing, and international competitions are frequently held there (details on ⓦ surfingportugal. com). **Horseriding** is superb in the Sintra hills. The Estoril Open in April/May draws **tennis** fans to the city (ⓦ millenniumestorilopen.com), and thousands of runners hit the streets for the **Lisbon Marathon** (ⓦ maratonaclubedeportugal.com), held in September/October.

Tickets

You can **buy tickets** for Lisbon's theatres and many concerts from the ticket desk in FNAC (ⓦ bilheteira.fnac. pt) in the Armazéns do Chiado shopping centre (see page 54), as well as from the main venues themselves. Online tickets can be purchased from ⓦ ticketline.sapo.pt or ⓦ blueticket. meo.pt.

Time

Portuguese **time** is the same as Greenwich Mean Time (GMT). Clocks go forward an hour in late March and back to GMT in late October.

Tipping

Service charges are included in hotel and restaurant bills. A ten-percent tip is usual for restaurant bills, and hotel porters and toilet attendants expect at least €0.50.

Toilets

There are very few **public toilets** in the streets, although they can be found in nearly all main tourist sights (signed variously as *casa de banho*, *retrete*, *banheiro*, *lavabos* or "WC"), or sneak into a café or restaurant if need be. Gents are usually marked "H" (*homens*) or "C" (*cabalheiros*), and ladies "M" (*mulheres*) or "S" (*senhoras*).

Tourist information

Lisbon's main **tourist office** is the Lisbon Welcome Centre at Praça do Comércio Loja 1 (see map page 26; daily 10am–6pm; ☏ 210 312 810, ⓦ visitlisboa.com), which can supply accommodation lists, bus timetables and maps. The main Portugal tourist office at Palácio Foz, Praça dos Restauradores (daily 9am–8pm; ☏ 213 463 314), is also helpful.

Tourist offices at the airport (see page 136) and at Santa Apolónia station (Tues–Sat 7.30am–9.30pm; ☏ 910 517 982) can help you find accommodation, as can a few smaller "Ask Me" kiosks dotted around town, like the one opposite Belém's Mosteiro dos Jerónimos (daily 10am–1pm & 2–6pm).

There are also tourist offices in all the main **day-trip destinations**: Sintra Turismo (see map page 110; daily 10am–6pm, until 7pm in August; ☎ 219 231 157, ⓦ cm-sintra.pt/turismo); Cascais Turismo (Praça 5 de Outubro; daily 9am–6pm; until 8pm in summer; ☎ 912 034 214, ⓦ visitcascais.com); and Caparica Turismo (Frente Urbana de Praias; Mon–Sat 9.30am–1pm & 2–5.30pm, Oct–March closed Sat; ☎ 212 900 071, ⓦ cm-almada.pt).

Travel agents

The well-informed Top Atlântico, Rua do Ouro 109 (ⓦ topatlantico.pt), Baixa, also acts as an American Express agent.

Water

Lisbon's **water** is technically safe to drink, though you may prefer bottled water. Inexpensive bottled water is sold in any supermarket, though tourist shops and restaurants charge considerably more.

Festivals and events

Carnival

February–March

Brazilian-style parades and costumes, mainly at Parque das Nações.

Peixe em Lisboa

March–April ⓦ peixemlisboa.com

Lisbon's annual fish festival takes place in Parque Eduardo VII and includes masterclasses by top chefs.

Sintra Music Festival

May or June
ⓦ festivaldesintra.pt

Performances by international orchestras and dance groups in and around Sintra, Estoril and Cascais.

Rock in Rio Lisboa

May or June (even years)
ⓦ rockinriolisboa.sapo.pt

Five-day mega rock festival in Parque Bela Vista, in the north of the city.

Santos Populares

June

June sees a series of city-wide events loosely based around three saints' days. Lisbon's main festival is for its adopted saint, Santo António. On June 12 there's a parade down Avenida da Liberdade followed by a giant street party in the Alfama, and the whole city is decked out in coloured ribbons with pots of lucky basil placed on window sills.

Lisboa Pride

June/July ⓦ ilga-portugal.pt

Lisbon's increasingly popular LGBTQ Pride changes venues, but in recent years has been held at Praça do Comércio.

Superbock Superrock

July ⓦ superbocksuperrock.pt

One of the country's largest rock festivals, with local and international

---

Public holidays

In addition to Christmas (Dec 24–25) and New Year's Day, public holidays include Shrove Tuesday (Feb/March); Good Friday (March/April); April 25 (Liberty Day); May 1 (Labour Day); Corpus Christi (late May/early June); June 10 (Portugal/Camões Day); June 12 (Santo António); Feast of the Assumption (Aug 15); Republic Day (Oct 5); All Saint's Day (Nov 1); Independence Day (Dec 1); Immaculate Conception (Dec 8).

bands at Parque das Nações and other venues.

NOS Alive

July ⓦ nosalive.com
Another big-time rock festival at the Passeio Marítimo de Algés, on the riverfront west of Belém, attracting big-name acts.

Jazz em Augusto

August ⓦ musica.gulbenkian.pt
Big annual (Jazz in August) festival at the Gulbenkian's open-air amphitheatre.

Christmas (natal)

The main Christmas celebration is midnight Mass on December 24, which is followed by a meal of *bacalhau*.

New Year's Eve (ano novo)

The best place for New Year's Eve is Praça do Comércio, where fireworks light up the riverfront, while the New Year's Day swim at Carcavelos Beach is a popular hangover cure.

Chronology

60 BC Julius Caesar establishes Olisipo as the capital of the Roman Empire's western colony.

711 Moors from North Africa conquer Iberia, building a fortress by the *alhama* (hot springs), now known as Alfama.

1147 Afonso Henriques, the first king of the newly established Portuguese state, retakes Lisbon from the Moors and builds a cathedral on the site of the former mosque.

1495–1521 The reign of Dom Manuel I coincides with the golden age of Portuguese exploration. So-called "Manueline" architecture celebrates the opening of sea routes. The 1494 Treaty of Tordesillas gives Spain and Portugal trading rights to much of the globe.

1498 Vasco da Gama returns to Belém with spices from India, which helps fund the building of the monastery of Jerónimos.

1581 Victorious after the battle of Alcántara, Philip II of Spain becomes Filipe I of Portugal, and Portugal loses its independence.

1640 Portuguese conspirators storm the palace in Lisbon and install the Duke of Bragança as João IV, ending Spanish rule.

1706–50 Under João V, gold and diamonds from Brazil kick-start a second golden age; lavish building programmes include the Aqueduto das Águas Livres.

1755 The Great Earthquake flattens much of Lisbon. The Baixa is rebuilt in "Pombaline" style, named after the Marquês de Pombal.

1800s Maria II (1843–53) rules with German consort, Fernando II, and establishes the palaces at Ajuda and Pena in Sintra. Fado becomes popular in the Alfama. Avenida da Liberdade is laid out.

1900–10 Carlos I is assassinated in Lisbon in 1908, while two years later, the exile of Manuel II marks the end of the monarchy and birth of the Republic.

1932–68 Salazar's dictatorship sees development stagnate. Despite massive rural poverty, elaborate "New State" architecture includes the Ponte

25 de Abril, originally named Ponte de Salazar.

1974 April 25 marks a largely peaceful Revolution. Former Portuguese colonies are granted independence, leading to large-scale immigration.

1986 Entry to the European Community enables a rapid redevelopment of Lisbon.

1990s Lisbon's role as Capital of Culture (1994) and host of Expo '98 helps fund a metro extension, the Ponte Vasco da Gama and the Parque das Nações.

2000–05 In 2004 Lisbon hosts the European Football Championships. Fado star Mariza brings the music to an international audience.

2005–2015 EU leaders sign the Lisbon Treaty on Dec 13, 2007, agreeing a draft constitution. Ten new upmarket hotels open in 2014, adding to Lisbon's burgeoning hotel scene.

2016 Socialist António Costa wins a controversial election with the support of the Communist party, vowing to "turn the page on austerity".

2018 Lisbon's Altice Arena hosts the Eurovision Song Contest, boosting an already record-high number of visitors to the city.

2020–2021 In common with most European cities, Lisbon suffers a series of lockdowns during the Covid pandemic, though rates in Portugal remained well below the EU average.

2022–2023 Tourist numbers bounce back to almost record numbers as Lisbon establishes itself as one of the most popular – and least expensive – city break destinations.

Portuguese

English is widely spoken in most of Lisbon's hotels and tourist restaurants, but you will find a few words of Portuguese extremely useful. Written Portuguese is similar to Spanish, though pronunciation is very different. Vowels are often nasal or ignored altogether. The consonants are, at least, consistent:

Consonants

c is soft before e and i, hard otherwise unless it has a cedilla – *açucar* (sugar) is pronounced "assookar".

ch is somewhat softer than in English; *chá* (tea) sounds like Shah.

j is like the "s" in pleasure, as is g except when it comes before a "hard" vowel (a, o and u).

lh sounds like "lyuh".

q is always pronounced as a "k".

s before a consonant or at the end of a word becomes "sh", otherwise it's as in English – Cascais is pronounced "Kashkaish".

x is also pronounced "sh"– Baixa is pronounced "Baisha".

Vowels

e/é: e at the end of a word is silent unless it has an accent, so that *carne* (meat) is pronounced "karn", while *café* is "caf-ay".

ã or õ: the tilde renders the pronunciation much like the French -an and -on endings

ão: this sounds something like a strangled "Ow!" cut off in midstream (as in *pão*, bread).

ei: this sounds like "ay" (as in *feito* – finished)

ou: this sounds like "oh" (as in *roupa* – clothes)

Words and phrases

Basics

sim yes

não no

olá hello

bom dia good morning

boa tarde/noite good afternoon/night

adeus goodbye
até logo see you later
hoje today
amanhã tomorrow
por favor/se faz favor please
tudo bem? everything all right?
está bem it's all right/OK
obrigado/a thank you (male/ female speaker)
onde where
que what
quando when
porquê why
como how
quanto how much
não sei I don't know
sabe...? do you know...?
pode...? could you...?
há...? (silent "h") is there...? there is
tem...? (pron. "taying") do you have...?
queria... I'd like...
desculpe sorry
com licença excuse me
fala Inglês? do you speak English?
não compreendo I don't understand
este/a this
esse/a that
agora now
mais tarde later
mais more
menos less
grande big
pequeno little
aberto open
fechado closed
senhoras women
homens men
lavabo/quarto de banho toilet/bathroom

Getting around

esquerda left
direita right
sempre em frente straight ahead
aqui here
ali there
perto near
longe far
Onde é... Where is ...
a estação de camionetas? the bus station?
a paragem de autocarro para... the bus stop for...

Donde parte o autocarro para...? Where does the bus to...leave from?
A que horas parte? (chega a...?) What time does it leave? (arrive at...?)
Pare aqui por favor Stop here please
bilhete (para) ticket (to)
ida e volta round trip

Common signs

aberto open
fechado closed
entrada entrance
saída exit
puxe pull
empurre push
elevador lift
pré-pagamento pay in advance
perigo/perigoso danger/ous
proibido estacionar no parking
obras (road) works

Accommodation

Queria um quarto I'd like a room
É para uma noite (semana) It's for one night (week)
É para uma pessoa (duas pessoas) It's for one person/two people
Quanto custa? How much is it?
Posso ver? May I see/ look?
Há um quarto mais barato? Is there a cheaper room?
com duche with a shower

Shopping

Quanto é? How much is it?
banco; câmbio bank; change
correios post office
(dois) selos (two) stamps
Como se diz isto em Português? What's this called in Portuguese?
O que é isso? What's that?
saldo sale
esgotado sold out

Days of the week

Domingo Sunday
Segunda-feira Monday
Terça-feira Tuesday
Quarta-feira Wednesday
Quinta-feira Thursday

Sexta-feira Friday
Sábado Saturday

Months

Janeiro January
Fevereiro February
Março March
Abril April
Maio May
Junho June
Julho July
Agosto August
Aetembro September
Outubro October
Novembro November
Dezembro December

Useful words

azulejo glazed, painted tile
cais quay
casa house
centro comercial shopping centre
estação station
estrada/rua street/road
feira fair or market
igreja church
jardim garden
miradouro viewpoint/belvedere
praça/largo square

Numbers

um/uma 1
dois/duas 2
três 3
quatro 4
cinco 5
seis 6
sete 7
oito 8
nove 9
dez 10
onze 11
doze 12
treze 13
catorze 14
quinze 15
dezasseis 16
dezassete 17
dezoito 18
dezanove 19

vinte 20
vinte e um 21
trinta 30
quarenta 40
cinquenta 50
sessenta 60
setenta 70
oitenta 80
noventa 90
cem 100
cento e um 101
duzentos 200
quinhentos 500
mil 1000

Food and drink terms

Basics

assado roasted
colher spoon
conta bill
cozido boiled
estrelado/frito fried
faca knife
garfo fork
grelhado grilled

Menu terms

pequeno almoço breakfast
almoço lunch
jantar dinner
ementa turística set menu
prato do dia dish of the day
lista de vinhos wine list
entradas starters
petiscos snacks
sobremesa dessert

Soups, salad and staples

açucár sugar
arroz rice
azeitonas olives
batatas fritas chips/french fries
caldo verde cabbage soup
fruta fruit
legumes vegetables
manteiga butter
massa pasta
molho (de tomate/piri-piri) tomato/chilli
sauce

omeleta omelette
ovos eggs
pão bread
pimenta pepper
piri-piri chilli sauce
queijo cheese
sal salt
salada salad
sopa de legumes vegetable soup
sopa de marisco shellfish soup
sopa de peixe fish soup

Fish and shellfish

atum tuna
camarões shrimp
carapau mackerel
cherne stone bass
dourada bream
espada scabbard fish
espadarte swordfish
gambas prawns
lagosta lobster
lulas (grelhadas) squid (grilled)
mexilhões mussels
pescada hake
polvo octopus
robalo sea bass
salmão salmon
salmonete red mullet
santola spider crab
sapateira crab
sardinhas sardines
tamboril monkfish
truta trout
viera scallop

Meat

alheira chicken sausage
borrego lamb
chanfana lamb or goat casserole
chouriço spicy sausage
coelho rabbit
cordeiro lamb
dobrada/tripa tripe
espetada mista mixed meat kebab
febras pork steaks
fiambre ham
fígado liver
frango no churrasco barbecued chicken
leitão roast suckling pig

pato duck
perdiz partridge
perú turkey
picanha strips of beef in garlic sauce
presunto smoked ham
rim kidney
rodizio barbecued meats
rojões cubed pork cooked in blood with
potatoes
vitela veal

portuguese specialities

açorda bread-based stew (often seafood)
arroz de marisco seafood rice
bacalhau à brás salted cod with egg and
potatoes
bacalhau a Gomes Sá dried cod with
potatoes
bacalhau na brasa dried cod roasted with
potatoes egg and olives
bife à portuguesa steak with a fried egg
caldeirada fish stew
cataplana fish, shellfish or meat stew
cozido à portuguesa boiled casserole of meat
and beans, served with rice and vegetables
feijoada bean stew with meat and vegetables
migas meat or fish in a bready garlic sauce
porco à alentejana pork cooked withclams

snacks and desserts

arroz doce rice pudding
bifana steak sandwich
bolo cake
gelado ice cream
pastéis de bacalhau dried cod cakes
pastel de nata custard tart
prego steak sandwich
pudim crème caramel

Drinks

um copo/uma garrafa de/da... a glass/
bottle of...
vinho branco/tinto white/red wine
cerveja beer
água (sem/com gás) (still/sparkling) water
fresca/natural chilled/room temperature
sumo de laranja/maçã orange/apple juice
chá tea
café coffee
sem/com leite without/with milk

Publishing Information

Sixth edition 2023

Distribution

UK, Ireland and Europe
Apa Publications (UK) Ltd; sales@roughguides.com
United States and Canada
Ingram Publisher Services; ips@ingramcontent.com
Australia and New Zealand
Booktopia; retailer@booktopia.com.au
Worldwide
Apa Publications (UK) Ltd; sales@roughguides.com

Special Sales, Content Licensing and CoPublishing

Rough Guides can be purchased in bulk quantities at discounted prices. We can
create special editions, personalised jackets and corporate imprints tailored to
your needs. sales@roughguides.com.
roughguides.com

Printed in China

This book was produced using **Typefi** automated publishing software.

Rough Guide Credits

Editor: Kate Drynan
Cartography: Katie Bennett
Picture editor: Piotr Kala
Layout: Pradeep Thapliyal

Original design: Richard Czapnik
Head of DTP and Pre-Press:
Rebeka Davies
Head of Publishing: Sarah Clark

Acknowledgements

Thanks for everyone who helped, especially Vitor Carrico, Heritage, Martinhal and 1908 hotels, Alex and Olivia. Thanks too to everyone at Rough Guides, especially Kate Drynan.

Help us update

We've gone to a lot of effort to ensure that this edition of the **Pocket Rough Guide Lisbon** is accurate and up-to-date. However, things change – places get "discovered", opening hours are notoriously fickle, restaurants and rooms raise prices or lower standards. If you feel we've got it wrong or left something out, we'd like to know, and if you can remember the address, the price, the hours, the phone number, so much the better.

Please send your comments with the subject line "**Pocket Rough Guide Lisbon Update**" to mail@uk.roughguides.com. We'll credit all contributions and send a copy of the next edition (or any other Rough Guide if you prefer) for the very best emails.

Photo Credits

(Key: T-top; C-centre; B-bottom; L-left; R-right)

Berardo Collection 85
Bogdan/Dreamstime.com 31
Calouste Gulbenkian Museum 94
Demetrio Carrasco/Rough Guides 18T, 96, 111
Eduardo Amaro/Santa Clara dos Cogumelos 47
Eleven 100
Franklin Heijnen/Flickr 69
iStock 2TL, 2BR, 4, 6, 10, 12T, 14T, 17B, 18C, 20T, 21C, 21C, 27, 37, 44, 51, 53, 79, 86, 87, 98, 105, 107, 109, 112, 114
Le Chat 75
Matthew Hancock 101
Miguel Manso/Pharmacia - Chef Felicidade restaurant 65

minemero 15T
Museu do Oriente 76
Natascha Sturny/Rough Guides 11T, 12B, 16B, 19T, 33, 40, 54, 56, 58, 89
Paulo Barata/Cantinho de Avillez 106
Piaras Ó Mídheach/Web Summit/Flickr 67
Rrrainbow 18C
Shutterstock 1, 2BL, 2C, 11B, 12/13T, 12/13B, 14B, 15B, 16T, 17T, 19C, 19B, 20C, 20B, 21C, 23, 24, 25, 29, 30, 34, 35, 41, 42, 45, 46, 48, 49, 57, 59, 62, 66, 68, 70, 71, 72, 77, 80, 81, 82, 91, 103, 115, 117, 118, 121, 122, 123, 124/125, 134/135

Cover: Torre de Belém **Shutterstock**

Index